W9-BAG-951

MYSTERIES, LEGENDS, AND UNEXPLAINED PHENOMENA

VAMPIRES

MYSTERIES, LEGENDS, AND UNEXPLAINED PHENOMENA

Astrology and Divination

ESP, Psychokinesis, and Psychics

Ghosts and Haunted Places

UFOs and Aliens

Vampires

Werewolves

Witches and Wiccans

MYSTERIES, LEGENDS, AND UNEXPLAINED PHENOMENA

VAMPIRES

ROSEMARY ELLEN GUILEY

Consulting Editor: Rosemary Ellen Guiley

CHELSEA HOUSE
PUBLISHERS

An imprint of Infobase Publishing

PALOS PARK PUBLIC LIB

VAMPIRES

Chelsea House
An imprint of Infobase Publishing
132 West 31st Street
New York NY 10001

Library of Congress Cataloging-in-Publication Data
Guiley, Rosemary.
  Vampires / Rosemary Ellen Guiley.
        p. cm. — (Mysteries, legends, and unexplained phenomena)
  Includes bibliographical references (p.   ) and index.
  ISBN-13: 978-0-7910-9398-6 (alk. paper)
  ISBN-10: 0-7910-9398-0 (alk. paper)
 1. Vampires. I. Title
  BF1556,G87 2008
  398.21—dc22

                                        2008009731

Chelsea House books are available at special discounts when purchased in bulk quantities for businesses, associations, institutions, or sales promotions. Please call our Special Sales Department in New York at (212) 967-8800 or (800) 322-8755.

You can find Chelsea House on the World Wide Web at http://www.chelseahouse.com

Text design by James Scotto-Lavino
Cover design by Ben Peterson

Printed in the United States of America

Bang EJB 10 9 8 7 6 5 4 3 2

This book is printed on acid-free paper.

All links and Web addresses were checked and verified to be correct at the time of publication. Because of the dynamic nature of the Web, some addresses and links may have changed since publication and may no longer be valid.

Contents

Foreword

Did you ever have an experience that turned your whole world upside down? Maybe you saw a ghost or a UFO. Perhaps you had an unusual, vivid dream that seemed real. Maybe you suddenly knew that a certain event was going to happen in the future. Or, perhaps you saw a creature or a being that did not fit the description of anything known in the natural world. At first you might have thought your imagination was playing tricks on you. Then, perhaps, you wondered about what you experienced and went looking for an explanation.

Every day and night people have experiences they can't explain. For many people these events are life changing. Their comfort zone of what they can accept as "real" is put to the test. It takes only one such experience for people to question the reality of the mysterious worlds that might exist beyond the one we live in. Perhaps you haven't encountered the unknown, but you have an intense curiosity about it. Either way, by picking up this book you've started an adventure to explore and learn more, and you've come to the right place! The book you hold has been written by a leading expert in the paranormal—someone who understands unusual experiences and who knows the answers to your questions.

As a seeker of knowledge, you have plenty of company. Mythology, folklore, and records of the past show that human beings have had paranormal experiences throughout history. Even prehistoric cave paintings and gravesites indicate that early humans had concepts of the supernatural and of an afterlife. Humans have always sought to understand paranormal experiences and to put them into a frame of reference that makes sense to us in our daily lives. Some of the greatest minds in history have grappled with questions about the paranormal. For example, Greek philosopher Plato pondered the nature of dreams and how we "travel" during them. Isaac Newton was interested in the esoteric study of alchemy, which has magical elements, and St. Thomas Aquinas explored the nature of angels and spirits. Philosopher William James joined organizations dedicated to psychical research, and even the inventor of the light bulb, Thomas Alva Edison, wanted to build a device that could talk to the dead. More recently physicists such as David Bohm, Stephen Hawking, William Tiller, and Michio Kaku have developed ideas that may help explain how and why paranormal phenomena happen, and neuroscience researchers like Michael Persinger have explored the nature of consciousness.

Exactly what is a paranormal experience or phenomenon? "Para" is derived from a Latin term for "beyond." So "paranormal" means "beyond normal," or things that do not fit what we experience through our five senses alone and which do not follow the laws we observe in nature and in science. Paranormal experiences and phenomena run the gamut from the awesome and marvelous, such as angels and miracles, to the downright terrifying, such as vampires and werewolves.

Paranormal experiences have been consistent throughout the ages, but explanations of them have changed as societies, cultures, and technologies have changed. For example, our ancestors were much closer to the invisible realms. In times when life was simpler, they saw, felt, and experienced other realities on a daily basis. When night fell, the darkness was thick and quiet, and it was easier to see unusual things, such as ghosts. They had no electricity to keep the night lit up. They had no media for constant communication and entertainment. Travel was difficult. They had more time to notice subtle things that were just beyond their ordinary senses. Few doubted their experiences. They accepted the invisible realms as an extension of ordinary life.

Today we have many distractions. We are constantly busy from the time we wake up until we go to bed. The world is full of light and noise 24 hours a day, seven days a week. We have television, the Internet, computer games, and cell phones to keep us busy, busy, busy.

We are ruled by technology and science. Yet, we still have paranormal experiences very similar to those of our ancestors. Because these occurrences do not fit neatly into science and technology, many people think they are illusions, and there are plenty of skeptics always ready to debunk the paranormal and reinforce that idea.

In roughly the past 100 years, though, some scientists have studied the paranormal and attempted to find scientific evidence for it. Psychic phenomena have proven difficult to observe and measure according to scientific standards. However, lack of scientific proof does not mean paranormal experiences do not happen. Courageous scientists are still looking for bridges between science and the supernatural.

My personal experiences are behind my lifelong study of the paranormal. Like many children I had invisible playmates when I was very young, and I saw strange lights in the yard and woods that I instinctively knew were the nature spirits who lived there. Children seem to be very open to paranormal phenomena, but their ability to have these experiences often fades away as they become more involved in the outside world, or, perhaps, as adults tell them not to believe in what they experience, that it's only in their imagination. Even when I was very young, I was puzzled that other people would tell me with great authority that I did not experience what I knew I did.

A major reason for my interest in the paranormal is precognitive dreaming experienced by members of my family. Precognition means "fore knowing," or knowing the future. My mother had a lot of psychic experiences, including dreams of future events. As a teen it seemed amazing to me that dreams could show us the future. I was determined to learn more about this and to have such dreams myself. I found books that explained extrasensory perception, the knowing of information beyond the five senses. I learned about dreams and experimented with them. I taught myself to visit distant places in my dreams and to notice details about them that I could later verify in the physical world. I learned how to send people telepathic messages in dreams and how to receive messages in dreams. Every night became an exciting adventure.

Those interests led me to other areas of the paranormal. Pretty soon I was engrossed in studying all kinds of topics. I learned different techniques for divination, including the Tarot. I learned how to meditate. I took courses to develop my own psychic skills, and I gave psychic readings to others. Everyone has at least some natural psychic ability and can improve it with attention and practice.

Next I turned my attention to the skies, to ufology, and what might be "out there" in space. I studied the lore of angels and fairies. I delved into the dark shadowy realm of demons and monsters. I learned the principles of real magic and spell casting. I undertook investigations of haunted places. I learned how to see auras and do energy healing. I even participated in some formal scientific laboratory experiments for telepathy.

My studies led me to have many kinds of experiences that have enriched my understanding of the paranormal. I cannot say that I can prove anything in scientific terms. It may be some time yet before science and the paranormal stop flirting with each other and really get together. Meanwhile, we can still learn a great deal from our personal experiences. At the very least, our paranormal experiences contribute to our inner wisdom. I encourage others to do the same as I do. Look first for natural explanations of strange phenomena. If natural explanations cannot be found or seem unlikely, consider paranormal explanations. Many paranormal experiences fall into a vague area, where although a natural cause might exist, we simply don't know what could explain them. In that case I tell people to trust their intuition that they had a paranormal experience. Sometimes the explanation makes itself known later on.

I have concluded from my studies and experiences that invisible dimensions are layered upon our world, and that many paranormal experiences occur when there are openings between worlds. The doorways often open at unexpected times. You take a trip, visit a haunted place, or have a strange dream—and suddenly reality shifts. You get a glimpse behind the curtain that separates the ordinary from the extraordinary.

The books in this series will introduce you to these exciting and mysterious subjects. You'll learn many things that will astonish you. You'll be given lots of tips for how to explore the paranormal on your own. Paranormal investigation is a popular field, and you don't have to be a scientist or a full-time researcher to explore it. There are many things you can do in your free time. The knowledge you gain from these books will help prepare you for any unusual and unexpected experiences.

As you go deeper into your study of the paranormal, you may come up with new ideas for explanations. That's one of the appealing aspects of paranormal investigation—there is always room for bold ideas. So, keep an open and curious mind, and think big. Mysterious worlds are waiting for you!

—Rosemary Ellen Guiley

Introduction

The supernatural world teems with weird creatures, monsters, and spirits. None is as shocking and frightening as the vampire. Neither living nor dead, it creeps out of its grave to suck the blood of the living. It's hard to find and harder to kill. For as long as human beings can remember, the vampire has terrorized the living world.

About 300 years ago, vampires came out of the shadows into the celebrity limelight. Since then they have filled newspapers, magazines, and books. They have taken to the stage to act, sing, and dance. More books, films, musicals, poems, and art have been created about vampires than most other supernatural creatures put together. Chances are, one of the first books you ever picked up about the supernatural was about vampires. And there's no end in sight to our love/fear affair with one of the deadliest creatures of all.

Do vampires really exist? There is no scientific proof of the **undead**, just as there is no scientific proof of ghosts, angels, demons, or any other being of the supernatural realm. Nonetheless, people have real supernatural experiences. You've probably had an experience or two that you can't explain and can't prove—but you know you had it.

That's the case with vampires. Vampires are indeed real, though not as depicted in novels and films. People have had terrifying encounters with vampires. Sometimes they have lived to tell their story, and sometimes they haven't, leaving the storytelling up to witnesses.

This book explores both familiar and little-known territory about the world's creepiest monster. You'll read about some true stories that you probably have never heard before, and you'll learn the surprising facts about different types of vampires. The focus here is on the supernatural and on portrayals of vampires in the entertainment industry. Blood crimes that are called vampire killings will not be discussed.

Chapter 1, "A Grave Matter," introduces and defines vampires. It looks at vampires throughout history and explores genuine living vampires as well as the ones from the grave. It tells the story of how vampires were "discovered." The sidebar "Vampires Around the World" describes the astonishing range of bizarre vampires. Glamorous they are not!

Chapter 2, "The Making of a Vampire," explores the many reasons why vampires are created and how. The sidebar, "Hey, Vampire Breath!," describes an amazing breed of vampire that kills just by breathing on people.

Do you think it's obvious how to recognize a vampire? Think again! Chapter 3, "It's A Dead Giveaway: Knowing a Vampire When You See One," talks about the telltale signs of the monster. Sometimes the signs aren't so obvious! Stand beside a vampire grave with a group of vampire hunters from centuries past, as they dig up a wooden coffin and examine the corpse for "vampire proof." Then, test your vampire knowledge against the sidebar, "True or False? Ten Things You Need to Know About Vampires."

Chapter 4, "Hunting Down the Vampire," tells what the real vampire hunters of the past—the "stakes for hire"—did to find and destroy their prey. Vampire hunting has to be one of the world's oddest, as well as disgusting and dangerous, jobs.

Vampires are not just confined to Europe and England. Not long ago they came to America, too. Chapter 5, "Vampires Invade New England," discusses the vampires who were believed to have killed people in the 1700s and 1800s—and how their bodies were dug up and sometimes turned into medicine. Can you imagine being prescribed a dose of vampire corpse in order to cure your ills?

Chapter 6, "The V-Files: Stranger-Than-Strange True Vampire Cases," documents some of the weirdest vampire stories on record. You may never see vampires the same way again! There's the vampire who drove around in his coffin like it was a car, the gangs who impersonated

Christopher Lee played Count Dracula, the world's best-known vampire, in several films beginning in the 1950s. He is credited with bringing charm and allure to the evil vampire's character. (Author's collection)

vampires in order to commit crimes, the lover who masqueraded as a dead vampire husband, and the vampires who infected an entire island of people with the trots.

Chapter 7, "Vlad the Bad," gives the lowdown on Romania's famous "vampire" prince. His name is linked to vampires, but did he really drink blood? There's no doubt, though, that he was one of the cruelest rulers of history. The "The Blood Countess" sidebar tells about Vlad's bloodthirsty female counterpart, Elizabeth Bathory, who believed that blood baths were her ticket to eternal youth.

Chapter 8, "From Count Dracula to the Vampire Lestat and Beyond," moves into fiction. How did the vampire become a permanent character in the literary world? How do fictional vampires compare to the real deal? Count Dracula became a model for all other fictional vampires to follow. Then Anne Rice's Lestat broke all the "rules." The sidebar, "Bats, Rats, and Shape-shifting," covers the vampire's many disguises.

Moving on from literature, Chapter 9, "The Entertaining Vampire," covers film and television. *Dark Shadows, Buffy the Vampire Slayer, Forever Knight*, and even reality television—nothing is off-limits when it comes to vampires! The more we see 'em, the more we love 'em! But wait—aren't we supposed to be *afraid* of vampires? The sidebar "Girls Makes Good Vampires, Too" lists famous female bloodsuckers.

Finally, Chapter 10, "The Vampire Underground," peeks into the shadowy world of "real living vampires," people who say they are vampires. They may or may not drink blood. They have their own secret societies, rules, and relationships. Your next-door neighbor might be one of them! This chapter explains what real vampires do, even though they cannot physically tolerate much blood drinking. The "But What About That Blood?" sidebar deals with that sticky problem, and "It's A Vampire Empire Out There" gives a thumbnail sketch of vampire fan clubs.

Even though this book covers a lot of territory, you may want to continue your study of vampires. Therefore, at the end you'll find some helpful resources, such as a list of Web sites and books, a timeline that covers milestones of vampire history, and a glossary of old and new terms that will help you master the lingo, especially in case you should ever find yourself having to make conversation with a vampire!

1

A Grave Matter

It's the early eighteenth century in a remote part of Transylvania, now part of Romania. A group of villagers huddles beneath a cold rain and watches while several strong men dig deeper into the wet, heavy earth of a grave. Everyone's attention is riveted to what lies within the ground. They are closing in on one of the most unholy creatures they know: the blood-sucking undead. People in the village have been dying, and a vampire is to blame.

At last a shovel strikes wood. A crude coffin is uncovered. With great effort the strongest men in the group pull it out to the surface. The villagers gather in a ring around it and fall silent. They are thankful that it is the job of the priest to deal with the corpse.

First, the villagers carefully examine the coffin on all sides. There are no obvious signs that it has been damaged. A wretched smell surrounds the long box. Even the dampening effects of the rain do not wash the smell out of the air. Onlookers cough, some of them violently. Most of them pull out their kerchiefs and cover their mouths. The kerchiefs are not enough to ward off the sickening smell.

When the coffin lid is pried off, a hellish stench blasts out into the air. People gag, double over, and choke. With tears streaming from his eyes, the priest bends down to peer into the contents of the coffin. Those around him who can stand it do so as well. As soon as they see what's inside, they cry out and stagger backwards. The corpse inside has a foul, blackish goo oozing from its nose and mouth. The muck is mixed with dark, red blood.

A cry goes up that carries throughout the village: "The vampire! The vampire! The vampire is found!"

DEAD PEOPLE WHO DON'T STAY IN THEIR GRAVES

The scene described above was replayed countless times in earlier centuries in remote parts of Eastern Europe, the Mediterranean, the Baltic areas, and western Russia. In these lands, beliefs were strong that the dead had the power to escape their graves and return to the living to attack them.

The restless dead were known as *vampires.* Not everyone who died became a vampire, but those who did were greatly feared. Vampires were powerful and deadly. They killed and terrorized the living, and it took special procedures to send them back into their graves permanently.

The vampire cult, as it was called, had evolved for centuries before it became known in other regions of the world. Once it was discovered in Western European nations—especially dominant countries such as England, France, Italy, and Germany—the vampire cult became the focus of fascination and curiosity. That interest still exists today. But how vampires are defined and what they are thought to be forms only a small element of the vampire cult. There is much more to the vampire than most people probably realize.

WHAT EXACTLY IS A VAMPIRE?

The answer to that question may seem simple. A vampire is a walking dead person who sucks the blood of the living.

While most vampires are indeed blood-drinkers, there are many kinds of vampires, and they feed off many things besides blood.

Figure 1.1 *Villagers uncover a vampire's grave and kill it by plunging a stake through its heart.* (Mary Evans Picture Library)

Vampires are known by many names. Being dead is not always a requirement—there are living vampires, too.

The simplest definition of a vampire is an entity that takes the life force. The term "entity" can include a spirit or a living being, and a spirit can include the ghost of a dead person, or a disembodied, nonhuman being, such as a demon.

Vampires exist in mythologies and folklore around the world, going back to ancient times. It seems human beings have always encountered supernatural forces, as well as magically empowered people who steal energy and life. Vampires take one's health and life, and they also take good fortune, beauty, wealth—whatever makes life good and pleasurable. Vampires also steal things that will make life more difficult. They will take the honey from bees, the milk from cows, or the leavening out of bread. Whatever they take from the living is food that keeps them going.

Vampires come in a lot of shapes and guises. For example, Philippine lore tells of vampires that are flying heads with sharp teeth. They zoom around at night, select sleeping victims, and tear out their entrails. They fly off, trailing the bloody guts behind them. Some vampires have specialties. There is a class of vampires known as "birth demons" because they prey upon newborn infants and their mothers. For more descriptions, see the sidebar, "Vampires Around the World."

Most of what people in Western culture believe about vampires comes out of Eastern Europe, the Baltic countries, Mediterranean lands, and to some extent, Russia. Especially in lands where Slavic populations were strong, the vampire flourished in folklore and in real life. People took vampires quite seriously as dangerous and life-threatening creatures. In all of these cultures, vampires were known by many different names. Their descriptions varied, but fundamentally they were all the same: They were the restless dead who escaped their graves and terrorized the living. They might have had one evil, vampirizing eye, like the *eretica* of Russian lore, or have been covered with feathers, like the Polish *upierzyca*. Their goal was the same: to take the life and life force from the living.

The word *vampire* was not documented until the late 1600s, when it appeared in French literature that described cases in Poland and Russia. It increased in usage in the 1700s, appearing in different languages in Europe, including English.

No one knows where the word came from. Scholars have suggested that it originated from Slavic terms such as *upir* and *upior*, which in turn come from a Turkish word, *uber*, for "witch." Some scholars think "vampire" came from a Serbian word, *bamiiup*, which may have Greek origins.[1] Another candidate is the Lithuanian word *wempti*, which means "to drink." The exact origin of *vampire* may never be known, but one thing is certain—just about everyone today has heard the term and knows what it means.

WHERE DO VAMPIRES COME FROM?

All types of vampires share two things in common: One, they are believed to be the cause of terrible things that happen to the living. Two, they personify human fear of death. Thus, the vampire explains why bad things happen to good people, and the vampire literally bites us with our deepest and darkest fear.

In many belief systems since ancient times, the dead were believed to be jealous of the living, because they were deprived of the pleasures of physical life. If they could find a way back into the world, they would come and try to have those pleasures again. They would steal those pleasures from the living. They would be unhappy and angry, too, like a bully who says, "If I can't have it, you can't have it, either," and they would suck away all life, love, and happiness.

Sometimes the dead came back because they were cursed, or because they couldn't find their way to the afterlife. Maybe they tried, and they got lost, or maybe they were prevented from reaching the afterlife because of terrible crimes and things they had done in life. All of those conditions, and more, could create a vampire.

In England, blood-sucking ghosts, called **revenants**, were described in written accounts dating to the twelfth century. They were not called vampires, because the word had not yet been invented. William of Newburgh was a twelfth-century English canon who included several of these stories in his written history of his times

Vampires Around the World

Vampires are found everywhere around the world. Some of them resemble the Eastern European vampire upon which Count Dracula was based. Some are both cannibals and blood-drinkers. Some are just plain weird. Here is an international sampling:

abchanchu This Bolivian vampire is disguised as a kindly old man who is lost. He sucks out the blood of victims while they sleep, or strikes them with a fatal disease.

baobhan sith A Scottish vampire fairy who likes to dress in green and attack men.

catacano A Cretan vampire that laughs hysterically for no known reason.

darg-diulai Irish vampire in the shape of a beautiful woman. Its name means "beautiful blood sucker."

erestun A Russian vampire, created when a dying person is possessed by an evil spirit. It eats the living.

hannya A Japanese vampire created when a demon possesses a woman and causes her to drink blood and eat human flesh.

incus This Vietnamese vampire has an antenna growing out of its nose that enables it to suck the blood out of victims.

jaracaca A Brazilian vampire that takes the form of a snake and attacks mothers and their newborns.

kathakano A Cretan vampire that must be killed by cutting off its head and boiling it in vinegar.

in England. There were so many, he said, that it would be tedious to include them all. One story involved a chaplain at Melrose Abbey, whose shrieking ghost returned after his death and attacked people

lampir This Bosnian vampire has wolf's hair and spreads plagues and epidemics.

mullo A Gypsy "living dead" who likes to harass people it hated during life. The mullo has long hair and fangs like tusks. It makes noisy disturbances at night, and strangles both animals and humans and drinks their blood.

nelapsi Slovakian vampire that can kill entire villages with the evil eye, suffocation, and blood-sucking.

pijawica Croatian vampire that cuts off its own head and carries it about under one arm.

quaxates This Mexican vampire makes women cry before it bites them.

sampiro Albanian vampire that wears a burial shroud and heeled shoes.

tlahuelpuchi A Mexican vampire witch that shape-shifts and attacks infants and their mothers.

uvengwa In West African lore, a vampire that has one huge eye in the center of its forehead like a cyclops.

vlokoslak A Serbian vampire who wears white clothes and shape-shifts into horses and sheep, and goes about day and night. It can be killed by cutting off its toes or pounding a nail through its neck.

xiang shi In Chinese lore, this vampire lives inside a corpse and feeds off other corpses and the living. It has red, staring eyes and long, crooked talons.

yuruga A Prussian vampire that smells so bad it can be detected up to a mile away.

at night. The ghost was seen coming and going out of the chaplain's grave. When the chaplain's body was dug up, it was bloody, as though it had been feasting on the living. The corpse was burned to ashes.

It cannot be said for certain exactly when the Slavic vampire came into being. Some historians trace the beginnings to the mythology of the ancient Slavs, who were sun-worshippers. They believed in a rather vague, vampiric demon who lived in the sky and vampirized the sun and moon by "eating them," that is, by causing eclipses. This demon also chased rain clouds and drained them of moisture, which is the life-blood of the sky.

Pagan Slavs believed the body was the tomb of the soul, and that after death, demons had the capability of invading the corpse and causing it to reanimate and wreak evil against the living. There were strict procedures for handling and burying corpses, lest demonic forces contaminate the living. The body was believed to be especially vulnerable during the time of decomposition, until the flesh was entirely wasted away.

The Slavic vampire cult grew until it reached its peak in about the fifteenth and sixteenth centuries. The growth was fueled in part by conversion to Christianity. The Church told pagan peasants that if they did not convert, they would become vampires after death and would be denied entry to heaven. Waves of epidemics and plagues also contributed to the vampire cult, for vampires were blamed for almost all diseases and illnesses.

THE VAMPIRE IS "DISCOVERED"

Up until the eighteenth century, the European vampire cult existed quietly. Large portions of countries were wild and remote, seldom visited by outsiders. Written accounts of vampire cases first appeared in European books, newspapers, and literature in the late 1600s and early 1700s, but by and large, the West slept peacefully, unaware of the dangers of the restless dead.

All that changed in 1742. The man who snapped Western attention to vampires was an Austrian military surgeon named Johann Fluckinger.

Fluckinger, a regimental field surgeon, was sent to villages near Belgrade to investigate reports of possible epidemics. Fluckinger discovered that the villagers blamed the restless dead. Peasants were digging up corpses and mutilating them to stop the dead from walking. Fluckinger and the soldiers with him were at once horrified and fascinated by these customs. He studied the vampire cult and wrote a report, which was published in German in 1732.[2]

The report was a best seller. It was quickly translated into French, English, and other languages. The word *vampire* was born. Civilized people were so shocked that they couldn't get enough information about vampires. Fluckinger's work was joined by at least a dozen other books on the mysterious and outrageous vampire cult.

One important text was *The Phantom World* by Dom Augustine Calmet. He was a Benedictine scholar in France who became fascinated by the vampire cult and by ghosts. Calmet collected material and published his two-volume work in French in 1746. It was translated into English in 1759. Calmet was open-minded about whether or not vampires were real or an illusion. If they were caused by demons, he said, then ultimately God allowed vampires to exist, because he allowed demons to exist. Criticism from skeptics and Calmet's religious training eventually caused him to reject the idea of real vampires.

Artists were not so hampered. It didn't take them long to jump on the vampire bandwagon with a great deal of enthusiasm. The image of the bloodthirsty dead was too good to pass up. The literary vampire was born, and it soon took on a life of its own.

VAMPIRES THAT AREN'T DEAD

While the restless dead seized the center stage, another kind of vampire was yet to be explored: the living vampire. Traditions of living vampires are just as old and widespread as those of dead or demonic vampires. Like vampiric entities, living vampires are known by many names. In the broadest sense, witches and sorcerers sometimes fit the bill of vampire. They were believed to be evil in nature and have the natural or magical ability to waste away living things. They could accomplish that by casting spells, throwing curses, sending evil looks, and attacking people, especially when they were asleep.

In African folklore, witches frequently indulge in vampirism. The witches leave their bodies and fly about in search of victims. They enter houses through the roofs and then enter the stomachs of sleeping persons. Inside, they use "secret spears" to stab the vital organs, such as the heart, liver, and lungs. They like to suck out hearts. They also suck off the essence of the victim's blood, that is, the blood's invisible life force and energy. The witches carry the blood essence to their gathering and put it in large pots. Because they have magical eyes, they can see the essence of the blood, but to ordinary eyes, the substance looks like water. The witches drink this brew. The victim immediately becomes ill and dies. If a witch is captured and confesses, and agrees to reform, she vomits up all the blood essence she has ever sucked.

Similar traditions of living vampire witches and sorcerers existed in Europe alongside the vampire cult of the undead. Living vampires were feared because they could walk around and take "power," that is, the life force, from anything.

In Romanian lore, female living vampires are dry in the body and red in the face before and after death. They leave their homes through their chimneys and return exhausted and in rags. Male vampires are bald, and after death, they grow a tail and hooves.

In Russian lore, living vampire sorcerers have the power to possess others, including the dead, who then become cannibals.

In the lore of the Karachay, the vampire sorcerers shape-shift with magical ointments. They mount brooms and fly up their chimneys in the form of a cat. At night, vampire sorcerers fly down chimneys and attack sleeping people and drink their blood. They are especially fond of children's blood. They go home at dawn and return to their normal shape.

ENERGY VAMPIRES

Some living vampires practice a form of vampirism that has nothing to do with blood: They suck energy. They are called **psi vampires** or psychic vampires. The ability to vampirize energy is not a new thing—human beings have been doing it for a very long time. In the magical arts, there are many methods for the draining of vitality from a person, animal, or even plant. These methods are a form of psychic vampirism. There are also methods for deliberately weakening someone's life force so that they become ill and suffer. That is called psychic attack.

The first person in the West to write about psychic vampirism was an Englishwoman, Violet Firth. She is better known by her magical name, Dion Fortune. When Fortune was a young woman in the early twentieth century, she had a job in which her mean boss psychically attacked her. She became progressively weakened and went through stages of exhaustion, mental confusion, and poor physical health. Fortune finally figured out what was going on and learned how to repel the attacks with magical and mental techniques. She wrote a guidebook on psychic vampirism called *Psychic Self-Defence*, which is still considered the leading book on the subject.

Psychic vampirism exists in the folklore of the undead, too. As mentioned earlier, vampires were known to steal far more than blood; they took whatever made life good and pleasurable. Psychic vampirism continues today in vampire cults, discussed further in Chapter 10, "The Vampire Underground."

There are many types of vampires, far more than the Count Dracula types made familiar by popular books and films, and there are many different causes of vampires, too.

The Making of a Vampire

In the 1600s, a horse kicked Johannes Cuntius, a resident of a village in Silesia (now part of Germany), in the groin. It was a fatal injury. Cuntius took to bed and never recovered. Just before he died, the 60-year-old man said he had sold his soul to the devil.

The people were shocked, for Cuntius had been a model, religious citizen. This confession had dire consequences for everyone. It meant that Cuntius would come back from his grave as a vampire. And come back he did, in the most devilish style.

Cuntius had been dead only one or two days when rumors circulated around his village that a demon called an incubus was appearing in his form. As a demonic vampire, Cuntius attacked women in the village and made noisy disturbances. Trampling noises resounded throughout his house at night, upsetting his widow. The noises were so severe that the entire house shook. Objects were flung about. Sleeping persons were beaten. Dogs barked all over town. Strange footprints, unknown as those of man or beast, appeared around the house. The attacks increased, and people were afraid to go to sleep at night.

Cuntius went on an even bigger rampage. He strangled old men, galloped around the house like a horse, wrestled with people, vomited fire, spotted the church's altar cloth with blood, bashed the heads of dogs against the ground, turned milk into blood, drank up supplies of milk, sucked cows dry, threw goats about, devoured chickens, and pulled up fence posts. Terrible smells and the sensation of foul, icy breath permeated the Cuntius house.

The vampire's reign of terror ended when his corpse was dug up and found to be in the vampire condition, fresh and exuding blood. The body was hacked to pieces and burned, and the ashes were cast into a river. The effects were immediate: Peace returned to the village.[1]

Whether or not the vampire Cuntius did all those deeds, or villagers conveniently blamed bad things on Cuntius, is difficult to know. But it was widely believed in those times in Europe that people did sell their souls to the devil—and the price was doom as a vampire.

Figure 2.1 *A Romanesque sculpture of a man making a pact with the devil. Such pacts were believed to turn people into vampires.* (Gianni Dagli Orti/Corbis)

CAUSES OF VAMPIRISM

Devil pacts were only one of numerous ways people believed that someone could be turned into a vampire after death. It's probably impossible to list all of the causes, because many beliefs were confined to small, local areas.

Almost any death that made people nervous or fearful could become a vampire case. Even without the devil pact confession, Cuntius would have been a vampire suspect just based on his freak, fatal accident alone. Widespread beliefs about the causes of vampirism existed through much of Europe, Russia, and parts of Asia. Here are the major ones:

Disease

In earlier times, people had no idea what caused illness and disease. They did not understand how bacteria infected people and spread through unclean conditions. Instead, plagues, epidemics, and all kinds of deadly illnesses were blamed on vampires. It was believed that when a plague or epidemic swept through an area, the victims who died were likely to come back as vampires. They would kill more people by infecting them with the same deadly illness. The only way to stop a plague was to find the vampire responsible, dig up its body, and mutilate or destroying it. Waves of tuberculosis were responsible for many vampire scares, even in America, and as late as the nineteenth century, as is discussed in the following chapter, "Vampires Come to New England."

Suicide

Taking one's own life is a spiritual crime in most religious and spiritual traditions. During the days of the vampire cult, a suicide victim was held to be rejected by God and so could not be buried in hallowed ground in the town church cemetery. The family of a suicide was socially and economically shunned. The punishment for anyone who took his own life was becoming a vampire. No wonder, then, that some families tried to hide a suicide—such as the family of a shoemaker in Breslau, Germany, in 1591.

The shoemaker, who is known only as the Breslau Vampire, killed himself by slitting his throat. No one knew why he did it. Fearing disgrace, the family tried to cover up the deed. It was customary then for families to wash and dress corpses and lay them out at home for a wake or public viewing. The shoemaker's family hired an old woman to handle the body and hide the wound. She was sworn to secrecy. The family told others that the shoemaker had died of a stroke. They allowed only the town priest to view the corpse before burial. The shoemaker was buried in the church cemetery in a fine ceremony.

But all was not well. The shoemaker did not rest peacefully. His ghost appeared both during the day and at night. It looked horrible and scared people. Rumors went around that there was something fishy about the shoemaker's death, and he had become a vampire. Nightmares were blamed on him. Women said the shoemaker vampire attacked them. Others said they were pinched, squeezed, bruised, and subjected to rackets of noise at night. Soon the vampire ghost appeared every day at sundown and attacked everyone in town.

Rumors increased and people began demanding that the shoemaker's body be dug up. Desperate, the family made up more lies. They said he hadn't really died of a stroke but had been fatally injured when he fell on a sharp rock. An awl—a sharp blade that he used in his trade—was in his pocket and had stabbed into him.

At last the townspeople prevailed. The body was dug up, eight months after death. As many expected, the corpse was in the vampire condition. Instead of destroying it, they aired it out for several days in a shed. The vampire attacks continued. The body was then buried beneath a gallows in the belief that the vampire would be imprisoned there. The attacks not only continued, they became nastier.

Finally, the shoemaker's widow confessed that he had taken his own life. The body was dug up again and was burned. The ashes were thrown into a river.

This remedy stopped the attacks. However, the shoemaker's maid soon died, and she, too, was said to return as a vampire and attack people. The townspeople wasted little time in digging her body up and burning it. Those attacks stopped, too.[2]

Violent and untimely death

Almost any peculiar or sudden death could be a cause of vampirism. In some parts of Europe, drowning was widely believed to be an

---

Hey, Vampire Breath!

Bad breath sometimes seems strong enough to knock you over, but can it actually kill you? According to folklore, there are real vampires that kill with bad breath.

One is the *nuckelavee*, a Scottish vampire whose fatal breath makes people and animals die instantly and causes plants to shrivel. This beast can lay waste to an entire landscape. The stolen life force becomes energy for the vampire. What's more, the *nuckelavee* does not resemble Dracula or other vampires. It has a half-human, half-horse body like a centaur. It has one eye that is always bloodshot and a pig-like snout that snorts steam. The *nuckelavee* causes droughts and epidemics and makes animals rush over cliffs and fall into the sea. It is allergic to rain and water.

The *yuki-onna* vampire of Japanese lore is prettier but just as deadly as the *nuckelavee*. *Yuki-onna* means "lady of the snow." This vampire takes the form of a beautiful maiden dressed in white. Her breath looks like frosty mist. She kisses her victims and breathes her killing breath into their bodies. Sometimes she appears only as mist and hovers over victims, who breathe her into themselves. When the vampire shapeshifts to mist, she can sneak into homes through cracks and under doorways. She attacks sleeping people. The *yuki-onna* also likes to stalk travelers who are stranded in snowstorms.

automatic vampire-maker. Other candidates included murders, deaths considered to be premature, and deaths due to accidents, especially under violent or tragic circumstances.

Improper burial

People have believed, since ancient times, that the dead must be treated properly and with respect, otherwise they will come back and harass the living. Around the world, people have followed what they consider to be the proper burial procedures. These include how a corpse is washed and dressed, how quickly it must be buried, where it will be buried, exactly how it will be transported to the burial place, and how the burial rites will be conducted. If mistakes are made, then the dead person is at risk of becoming a vampire. In parts of Eastern Europe, for example, if an animal jumps over a corpse before burial, it is a very bad sign that the deceased may return as one of the undead.

Attacks by vampires

In the days of the vampire cult, it was believed that if you were attacked by a vampire while you were alive, and then died soon thereafter, you, too, became a vampire. Since this taint or curse applied to deadly infectious diseases, that was how people explained why entire families and even villages fell ill: They were attacked by the vampire dead.

Vampire attacks could be random, too. Take the case of Arnod Paole, a Serbian solder who was sent to Greece in the early 1700s for a tour of duty. While there, Paole learned of the local beliefs about vampires. To his alarm, he discovered that his company was stationed in an area said to be heavily haunted by vampires. The possibility of a vampire attack scared Paole, and he thought about it constantly.

One night, Paole became convinced that a vampire had attacked him. In panic, he followed a local custom: He went to the grave where he believed the vampire lived, dug up the corpse, and mutilated it. He also ate some of the grave dirt because, according to lore, this would help to prevent a vampire's victim from becoming a vampire, too.

Figure 2.2 *An engraving of a vampire killed with a stake.* (Bettmann/Corbis)

Despite these tactics, Paole could not stop worrying that he might become a vampire. He fell into a terrible depression. Even going home and marrying a Serbian girl did not lift his spirits. Paole confided in his bride that he believed he was now cursed, and he was also doomed to die before his time.

Fate took its course. In 1732 Paole fell off a hay wagon and broke his neck. He survived for several days before dying.

Within a month, Paole was back as a vampire. The locals said he attacked both people and their livestock. Four persons died. Those who survived complained of feeling exhausted, as though their very blood had been drained.

For 10 days Paole terrorized the living. Then his body was dug up and found to be full of what looked like fresh blood. It oozed from his lips. The church sexton cried out, "So, you have not wiped your mouth since last night's work!" Onlookers fainted.

Paole's body was driven through with a great stake. It was reported that a huge stream of blood gushed up, like a spring. That put an end to Paole the vampire. His four victims were dug up and staked as well, to prevent them from attacking the living.[3]

3

It's a Dead Giveaway: Knowing a Vampire When You See One

The year: 1750. The place: Serbia. The problem: A vampire is on the loose.

People in a tiny village fall suddenly ill and die. The rate of death increases. Fear hangs over the homes. People are afraid to go out, to see others. No one knows who will be next. The village officials gather together to discuss what to do. They all agree that there is only one course of action: The vampire must be found and killed.

The officials must locate the person who has died who is not staying in the grave. They put together a list of suspects whose graves will be opened. They will examine their remains for the telltale signs, the proof, of vampirism.

The officials know exactly what they are looking for. Let the grave openings begin!

SIGNS OF RECOGNITION OF THE UNDEAD

How did people know a vampire when they saw one?

Vampire hunters knew exactly what they were looking for and where to find it. Vampires were dead—or rather, undead, since they returned from the grave to the living world. The only place to find vampires was in a grave. Therefore, bodies of the dead had to be dug up and then examined for certain signs that the corpse of a dead person was clinging to an unnatural life.

Since vampires fed themselves on the blood and life force of the living, there would be evidence of that. People knew that corpses decomposed, that the flesh rotted off the bones, and after a very long time, the bones turned to dust. Therefore, a vampire that was sucking the vitality off the living would be in an unnatural state for the dead. The corpse would not be properly decomposed. People back then did not understand that rates of decomposition can vary quite a bit, depending on soil and humidity conditions, and even the health, age, and manner of death of the person. Anything that didn't look normal to vampire hunters indicated vampirism.

Here are the major signs taken as proof of vampirism:

Fresh flesh

Lack of decay and decomposition was the primary proof. A corpse in the vampire condition might look as though the person were asleep and not dead or look at least reasonably fresh, with no rot. The skin would be pinkish and ruddy. The hair and nails would look shiny and good. The body would be bloated, as though the corpse had feasted like a glutton. Amazingly, the corpse might even feel warm to the touch.

Actually, decomposing bodies often look pink and reddish in the skin. Small blood vessels called capillaries break, and blood spreading through the corpse can give skin a false healthy glow. Blood pools according to gravity, too.

Nails begin to slough off after death. Sometimes the nail beds beneath the nails were mistaken for new nail growth. Hair has varying rates of decay. Decomposition can also generate gases that temporarily make a corpse bloated and feel warm.

Sometimes, naturally decaying bodies do not smell bad. This also was seen as a sign of vampirism. However, old accounts of grave openings describe plenty of smelly bodies. A stinking corpse that had other sure signs of vampirism would be judged a vampire, smell or no.

Presence of blood

Many old accounts of unearthed vampires describe the fresh blood that oozed out of corpses' mouths, ears, and noses—in fact, out of any body openings. If the blood was bright red instead of dark and muddy looking, so much the better: This proved that the vampire was gorging itself on the blood of the living. It was so full that it couldn't even keep all the blood in its stomach.

In fact, the gases that build up in decomposition can push the corpse's own blood out of body openings. The color depends on many factors. Corpse blood can sometimes appear bright like the blood of the living.

Flexible limbs

People observed that after death, bodies go rigid and stiff—a condition called rigor mortis. So, if a corpse had flexible, or flaccid, limbs, that meant it was unnaturally alive. In earlier times, burials were often swift, while corpses were still rigid. People did not know that rigor mortis disappears after a while, and bodies become flaccid again.

Movement inside the coffin

If a corpse was not found laid out in the coffin as it was at the time of burial, it was assumed to have the ability to leave and re-enter the grave—a vampire trick.

Some historians have thought that evidence of movement indicated that a person had been buried alive. It is likely that in the past, some people presumed to be dead were not, but, rather, were in deep comas. It is possible that some may have regained consciousness after burial and tried desperately to claw their way out. The most likely explanation for movement in the coffin, though, is decomposition. Shifting gases inside a corpse can cause the body to move, making it look like the body still has life.

True or False?
Ten Things You Need to Know About Vampires

Think you know the real truth about vampires? Test yourself against this list of most common beliefs:

1 **Vampires are destroyed by sunlight.** False. This is pure fiction, introduced in the film *Nosferatu* (1922), in which the vampire disintegrates when struck by the rays of the morning sun. Folklore beliefs about vampires hold that they can be out at any time of day or night—though they do like to prowl around more at night when their victims are sleeping.

Figure 3.1 *Max Schreck as Count Orlock in* Nosferatu. (Author's collection)

2 **Vampires are repelled by garlic.** True. In fact, garlic is an ancient remedy against anything evil. Some of our early beliefs about garlic may have to do with its ability to benefit the immune system. Thus, a person might be more resistant to the diseases blamed on vampires.

3 **Vampires cast no reflection in mirrors and have no shadows.** False. These ideas are fiction dramatized in Bram Stoker's *Dracula*. There is plenty of folklore about mirrors as portals for ghosts and demons, but nothing in folklore says that vampires have no reflection. The same applies to shadows. Stoker said the vampire has no shadow because it has no soul. This does not appear in vampire folklore. However, since most vampires are spectral like ghosts, they are unlikely to cast shadows anyway.

4 **Vampires have supernormal strength.** Partially true and partially false. Early cases tell of vampires rampaging through homes, upsetting objects, throwing things about, and bashing people and animals around. That would suggest unusual strength. But the superhuman abilities portrayed in fiction, such as in Anne Rice's *Vampire Chronicles*, are just that—fiction.

5 **Vampires are immortal.** False. In fiction they are immortal—until someone does them in. Real vampires are spirits, not resurrected corpses. They can be sent away or destroyed, according to belief, by destroying the corpse that houses them. They may even go away on their own after a while.

6 **Vampires are weakened by holy objects such as crosses and Eucharists.** True. The Christian church taught pagans to use Christian symbols as the way to fight evil. Other things work, too, including holy objects of other faiths. Folklore around the world holds that iron will weaken anything evil—or anything in spirit form.

(continues)

(continued)

7   **Vampires can shape-shift.** True. Vampires can take just about any form they want, according to lore. They can become animals, birds, bats, insects, and even mist. Their shape-shifting enables them to gain entry into homes and places where they can attack the living.

8   **Vampires have to sleep in coffins.** False. This is an invention of fiction. Even the granddaddy of fictional vampires, Count Dracula, did not sleep in a coffin, but in a box of dirt from his homeland. Having to cart his dirt around with him is fiction, too.

9   **Vampires must be killed with a stake.** False. Staking a corpse was the most common means of destruction. But peasants were creative, too. They shot vampires, stabbed them, cut them up into pieces, and burned them to ashes.

10 **Anything can become a vampire.** True. In folklore, animals can become vampires. But how about vegetables? Ever hear of a vampire head of lettuce or a vampire turnip? In Gypsy lore, vegetables that are not eaten and left to go bad turn into vampires. They don't drink blood, but they rattle around a house at night, making disturbances. Similarly, even tools can become vampires. Gypsy lore holds that tools that are not properly cared for and stored will become unhappy and turn into vampires at night, making great rackets.

Chewed burial clothes and body parts

If an unearthed body had a burial shroud or clothing that looked chewed, or hands and fingers that looked gnawed, vampire hunters took it as a sign of a hungry vampire. It simply couldn't wait to get out of the coffin to eat.

In 1345 a European woman said to be a witch died. Being a witch, she could not be buried in a churchyard, so her body was dumped into a ditch. This improper burial turned her into an angry vampire. She returned in the forms of demonic beasts, attacking and killing people. When the villagers dug her up, she was found to have chewed and swallowed one-half of the cloth that was wrapped around her face. When the cloth was pulled away, it was bloody. The witch was staked in the heart, but the vampire was not killed. Instead, according to lore, the stake became her weapon. Every night she came back from her grave and used the sharp stake to kill the living. The witch was dug up again and burned, putting an end to her.[1]

Rude noises

Vampire corpses that were pressed, cut, or staked sometimes emitted hideous sounds. This was taken as the final proof of vampirism—an infernal protest against being put to death once and for all. European accounts tell of vampires moaning, shrieking, and screaming as stakes were pounded into their hearts. While that sounds dramatic and has certainly fueled many a novel and movie, there is a natural explanation.

Once again, decomposition is the culprit, not vampirism. A decaying body creates gases that build up inside, especially in cavities in the body. A stake is like a pin in a balloon. When it punctures the corpse, air and gases rush out and make noises as they do so.

One particular "vampire" noise was common enough to be given a name: *vresket*. This Croatian word refers to the special sound made in the throat when a vampire corpse is staked. The sound comes from gases rushing past the glottis, which is involved in speech.

One of the noisiest vampires on record is a man named Myslata, a herdsman who lived in Bohemia (now part of Germany) in the 1300s.

The cause and circumstances of Myslata's death are not known, but after death, he returned as a vampire. According to accounts, he cried out the names of people in his village, and then they died within eight days. Alarmed by this supernatural death omen, the villagers dug up Myslata's body and drove a stake through its heart.

This did not stop the vampire. He got uglier, appearing in a more hideous form at night. He attacked sleeping people and suffocated several of them to death. It was even claimed that the vampire frightened others to death. He supposedly told the villagers that the stake that was put through his heart did not hurt him but would be useful to him in keeping dogs away.

The desperate villagers dug up Myslata's body a second time. The village executioner drove several more stakes through the vampire's heart. The vampire screamed and shrieked the entire time. While the vampire still screamed, the executioner took the body and burned it. The vampire stopped screaming. The attacks and deaths also came to a halt.[2]

LIVING VAMPIRES

What about living vampires, or people said to be vampires because of their powers in witchcraft or sorcery? How did people in earlier times recognize them? Living vampires didn't walk about in Goth clothing or hang out in vampire clubs like present-day living vampires.

Sometimes such people were identified by heredity. Every village and town had certain families who were known for their magical skills and their reputation for spell-casting. In some places, such magical people were called vampires or vampire witches.

According to lore, certain people are just fated to be born as vampires. Some are readily identified at birth by physical oddities such as teeth already showing or a spine deformity that resembles a tail. If a child is the seventh child of seven children who are all the same sex, he or she is fated to be a living vampire. In Romanian lore, if a pregnant woman does not eat salt—a protector against all things evil—her child will be born a living vampire.

Figure 3.2 *Bulbs of garlic hang near a window. Garlic is believed to repel vampires.* (Adrianna Williams/zefa/Corbis)

Appearances often made a difference. Anyone who looked strange by local standards, such as having red hair when most of the locals were brown-haired, could be labeled as a type of vampire. Such a person might be suspected of causing any sort of vampirism or vampiric phenomena, such as bad weather, bad luck, bad marriages, bad harvests, and even bad health and death.

In particular, a living vampire might have unusual eyes. Throughout history, it's been said that certain people are born with the ability to *overlook*, that is, cause misfortune merely by looking at someone a certain way. The **evil eye** is widespread in folklore belief. It is a vampirizing eye, because it takes away whatever a person considers good and blessed.

In some beliefs, being born with a caul means a person is destined to be a witch, sorcerer, caster of the evil eye, or vampire. A caul is part of the inner fetal membrane containing amniotic fluid. It normally comes off during childbirth, but sometimes a child is born with it still covering the head, and sometimes the body. A person born with the caul was usually considered special in a magical way.

For example, the Kashubs are an old Slavic sect that still exists. Some have immigrated to Canada. They have long traditions of living vampires, who are identified at birth. One kind, the *vjesci*, is born with the caul. The *vjesci* can live a normal life if the caul is dried, turned into ashes, and fed to the child at age seven. This will prevent evil vampire powers from taking hold of the person. After death, the body requires special handling in order to prevent the person from returning as a ghostly vampire.

The second kind of Kashubian vampire is the *opji*, who is born with teeth already showing. The *opji* is dangerous and will harm others with the evil eye if he becomes mad. A mad *opji* gets very red in the face. The Kashubs have an expression to describe any angry person: He is "red as a vampire."

Vampire lifestylers—people who want to become vampires like those in fiction—are another type of living vampire. They have their own identifying characteristics, discussed in Chapter 10, "The Vampire Underground."[3]

Hunting Down the Vampire

Long before there were cowboys and gunslingers in the Wild West of America, there were cowboys of sorts in remote parts of Eastern Europe. They rode horses, carried unusual weapons, and came into town looking for action. Their specialty: killing vampires.

Like many gunslingers from the Old West, who were hired guns, vampire killers were hired to help out a town. They were, well, the hired stake. Usually, the local villagers did the dirty work of killing vampires, but sometimes they were unsuccessful. They could not find the vampire corpse, or it kept coming back from the grave after they tried to kill it. When either of those things happened, it was time to call in a professional.

A vampire killer rode into a village on a fine horse, advertising that he was paid handsomely for his work. His appearance told the local people he was powerful. They feared him almost as much as they did the undead entity that was stalking the town. For the next day or so, the vampire killer would conduct mysterious rituals to find and destroy the vampire.

During the height of the vampire cult, professional vampire killers made a good living ridding a town of vampires. What made a person a genuine vampire killer? There were no classes or schools for vampire killers. How did they learn their trade, and how did they hunt and kill their prey?

BORN TO KILL VAMPIRES

Most vampire killers were born into their trade. Like witches, spell casters, and sorcerers, certain people were believed to be born with magical ability. In the case of vampire killers, their special calling was the ability to see invisible vampires and slay them. In a way, they were the early versions of Buffy the vampire slayer. They carried on traditions, usually handed down in their families. What made them different from Buffy is that they were always men, never women. Their fathers and grandfathers before them were vampire hunters, and they were trained by their **elders**. If they married and had sons, then those boys might grow up to be vampire hunters, too.

Some vampire hunters born into their calling were not descended from special bloodlines. Rather, they were born under special circumstances. For example, persons born on a Saturday were widely believed to possess magical powers that enabled them to see spirits and kill vampires. Why Saturday? Because it is the sixth day of the week, the day that God rested from his creation of the cosmos, according to the Bible. Twins born on a Saturday are especially powerful.

Another special vampire killer was the *dhampir*. He was the child of a woman and her dead vampire husband. Many people in those times believed that the dead could come back to conceive children. More likely, a woman had a child out of wedlock and blamed it on a dead husband. In some lore, *dhampirs* can pass on their magical skills to their own sons, but they cannot teach their skills to outsiders.

Regardless, the *dhampir* was the most fearsome vampire hunter in all of Europe. *Dhampir* is a Slavic term for "devil's partner." The name does not mean the *dhampir* is evil, but rather that he possesses magical powers that enable him to combat evil. The *dhampir* was so powerful that he could kill all the vampires anywhere in the world. Fortunately for the *dhampir*, transportation was limited in those days, and so he usually had to fight only those vampires in his area. Contrary to popular belief, *dhampirs* didn't always have to stake a body to kill a vampire, but their job was never dull.[1]

CALLING IN THE HUNTER: A TYPICAL CASE

In the Serbian village of Svojdrug, people suddenly complain of being attacked at night while they sleep. A vampire is on the loose. A number of people have died lately, but there is no obvious suspect as to the identity of the vampire. It might even be someone who has been dead a long while.

The villagers dig up three bodies, but none of them are in the "vampire condition." Meanwhile, the attacks worsen. Two people have died. Cattle are being attacked, too. Something must be done quickly. They summon a *dhampir*. His fee is high and all of his expenses must be paid. In return for killing the vampire, he will be given a good meal and the best livestock that the village has to offer.

The Hunt

The *dhampir* arrives on a huge white horse. He knows that people expect a performance as well as a vampire slaying, so he makes a big show of his hunt. He will make certain that he earns his fee. He is stern and doesn't say much. When he gives instructions, he expects others to follow them silently and without question.

He announces that the air stinks. He smells something that others do not—the stench of a vampire. Then he takes off his shirt, holds up the sleeve, and looks through it, scanning the village. If he chooses, he may allow others to look through the sleeve. They, of course, will see nothing unusual. He will see the vampire.

The *dhampir* plots a trap to ambush the vampire. Vampires like to strangle cattle, so he will use the cattle to lure the vampire out into the open. He tells the villagers to take all of their cattle down to the river to stand near the flowing water. This will help to protect them against the vampire. Folklore holds that running water is pure, and vampires, being evil, cannot come near it. He asks for a gun and a cowbell. He hides near the cattle and rings the cowbell. Soon the invisible vampire arrives. The *dhampir* waves the gun around and shoots into the air. He shouts that he has killed the vampire. The villagers bring a bucket of water and pour it onto the spot where the *dhampir* says the vampire fell. The water will purify the earth.

Even though they are afraid of the *dhampir*, the villagers will not necessarily just take his word that the vampire has been killed. They will want some kind of proof through identification. The *dhampir* does not know anyone in the village, but he must provide some information that points to a dead person. He may say the vampire is a man or a woman, or describe a nationality, or other features. The identification will be general but enough to satisfy the villagers. The *dhampir* is searched for hidden objects to prevent falsification of evidence.

On some occasions, the *dhampir* says he cannot kill the vampire, but will send it away from the village. He orders it to get out. This solution is not an ideal one, however, because there is always the possibility that the vampire will return.

After the vampire has been dispatched, it is time to eat and be paid. Women in the village have worked all day to prepare a meal of the best they have to offer. The men bring forth the cattle they will give the *dhampir*. Afterward, he moves on.

His next job is at a village where another unknown vampire has been attacking and killing people. This time, his tactics will be different.

After scanning the village through his sleeve, the *dhampir* announces that he will search the graves in the cemetery. He scatters ashes and salt around some of the graves. The vampire will leave telltale footprints when it goes in and out of its grave. The *dhampir* waits. He also looks for other signs of vampires, such as balls of blue-white light that float over the ground.

After two nights, his vigil is successful. There is a disturbance in the ashes and salt around one of the graves. The *dhampir* orders the grave to be opened. The body inside has signs of vampirism. He takes a gravedigger's shovel—the best for the job—and uses it to drive a huge stake through the vampire's chest. He slashes the soles of its feet. Just to be certain the job is done, he cuts off the corpse's head and tucks it under one armpit. All of these measures will keep the vampire in its grave. It will not be able to walk the earth and attack the living.

Figure 4.1 *An early seventeenth-century Vampire Killing Kit from England. The kit includes a pistol, silver bullets, a cross, and vials of herbs and potions to ward off vampires.* (Ken Schmidt/Kerville Daily Times/AP)

Sometimes the *dhampir* will order the corpse cut up and burned to ashes. The ashes will be scattered in running water. This thoroughly destroys the physical vehicle that keeps the vampire alive in the grave, and thus destroys the vampire itself.

And so the job goes. Sometimes there is a lot of work, such as when an epidemic sweeps through an area and many people die. At least one or more of them will be vampires, causing other people to die, too. Sometimes there is very little work. Since the vampire hunter is paid in livestock, he is usually assured of feeding his family for a long time.

ADDITIONAL WAYS TO HUNT VAMPIRES

Vampire hunters—*dhampirs* and others—used a variety of ways to identify vampires. One telltale sign was the condition of a vampire's grave, which was often sunken more than other graves or had holes near it. These were signs of the vampire going in and out of the burial place.

Certain animals were believed to have vampire-hunting powers. A white horse, especially one that had never stumbled, would not be able to step over the grave of a vampire. The technique worked even better if a young boy rode the horse, for his purity would affect the results.

Similarly, a black dog with four eyes, that is, eye-shaped marks above its eyes, would be able to sniff out a vampire's grave. If villagers were lucky enough to capture a white wolf, the wolf also would sense the grave and destroy the vampire by strangling it.

DESTROYING THE VAMPIRE

When a vampire corpse was discovered, it was prepared for execution, usually by staking. The corpse was covered with a cloth to avoid sprays of the vampire's blood. Anyone unlucky enough to be hit by a vampire's blood would either go mad or die instantly and probably become a vampire, too.

More Vampires Around the World

Here are more intriguing vampires from international lore:

afrit In Arabian lore, a man who is murdered may become a re-vengeful vampire that forms from his blood.

brahmaparusha An Indian vampiric demon who wears a wreath of intestines around his head. The vampire gnaws the flesh off the head of his victim and drinks the blood from a skull.

callicantzaros A Greek vampire with long and sharp talons. It comes out from the underground only between Christmas and January 7.

eretik In Russian lore, a cannibal vampire.

hantu penanggalan In Malaysian lore, a bodiless head that sucks out entrails.

kozlak A Dalmatian vampire that enters homes at night and makes loud disturbances, like a poltergeist.

leyak A Balinese sorcerer who can shape-shift into a vampire demon and cause death and destruction.

mwere This Kashubian vampire is the spirit of a child who died un-baptized. It suffocates and chokes its sleeping victims.

nagasjatingarong Indonesian vampire that kills husbands.

obur Karachay shape-shifting witch vampire that flies on brooms and drinks blood.

pricolici Romanian vampire that eats the sun and moon and sucks the blood of its living relatives.

(continues)

(continued)

raksasa Indian vampire that gets into people while they eat and drives them insane. It attacks newborn children and drinks their blood; attacks more often when the moon is new or dark. The raksasa also shape-shifts into dogs, eagles, vultures, owls, and cuckoos.

strix Greco-Roman "screech owl" vampire that attacks children for their blood and flesh.

upir Russian vampire that attacks its living friends and family by hugging them hard, then sucking their blood.

vukodlak Slavic vampire created when a demon enters a corpse and reanimates it. The vukodlak leaves the grave and attacks the living for blood. It sleeps with one eye open and has long nails and hair. It's name means "wolf's hair."

The stake was believed to pin the corpse in the grave and prevent the vampire from escaping. The stake was not always pounded into the heart. It was sometimes pierced into the head or belly. The stake had to be made of a certain kind of magical wood, which had special power. Depending on the local beliefs—and the type of trees in the area—the stake might be aspen, hazelwood, rowan, hawthorn, maple, blackthorn, whitethorn, oak, or juniper. The stake was not always pounded in with a hammer. A preferred tool was a gravedigger's shovel, which was believed to possess the holy power of God. Sometimes other sharp objects, such as iron nails, iron spikes, and needles were used instead of a stake. In folklore, iron has power over spirits, weakening them.

A staked vampire corpse was often washed with boiling wine or scorched with a hot iron. Then the coffin was filled with vampire repellent such as garlic or poppy seeds. Just in case the vampire managed to survive, the garlic would keep it bound in the grave. The tiny seeds would provide food. According to lore, the vampire would have to eat one seed at a time, and eat them all, before it could leave the grave again.

Sometimes vampire hunters might take more extreme measures. There were cases known where vampires that had been staked were not killed. They were said to pull their stakes out and use them as weapons against the living. The more damage done to a corpse, the less likely the vampire would survive. Sometimes the hunters would cut off the head of the vampire, and, like the *dhampir* mentioned earlier, tuck it under an armpit, or underneath the buttocks or feet. The severed head was stuffed with garlic, coins, or stones. Slashing the bottoms of feet and the tendons in the legs prevented the vampire from walking. Cutting off the arms prevented it from attacking.

The mutilated corpse was reburied, but with extra dirt between the head and the torso. It was thought best not to rebury the corpse in the same grave, but to relocate it so as to disorient the vampire. The best location was at a crossroads, which would be the most confusing place of all. Sometimes the head and body parts were reburied in separate locations, or the body or body parts might be tossed into a river. In folklore, water is pure: Running water will cleanse and purify anything evil.

The most effective method of killing a vampire was to destroy the body by burning it to ashes, and also scattering them into running water. The job of burning was particularly unpleasant and difficult. The village hangman or executioner usually had to do it. Bonfires were not hot enough to completely burn up a body. The hangman had to keep hacking the body into smaller pieces in order to get them to burn. The difficulty of burning a body was taken as a sure sign of vampirism.[2]

HOLY REMEDIES

Vampire beliefs and ways of killing vampires originated in pagan folklore. They existed before villages were converted to Christianity. When Christianity was introduced to remote parts of Eastern Europe, the church authorities told the pagans that the only effective ways to deal with vampires were holy ones. That is how the cross or crucifix, as well as holy water and the Eucharist (consecrated bread), became part of the vampire hunter's toolkit. The church imposed other rules on vampire hunting, too. Priests told villagers that they were the only ones who could officiate at the opening of graves, and over time, the church tried to discourage vampire hunting and grave openings by having hunters arrested and punished.

Methods of killing vampires were not always successful the first time, and this applied to holy remedies as well as the traditional pagan ones. That's what happened in the case of Milos Rakovic, a Serbian man who died in 1836. Suspected of being a vampire, his body was dug up three times.

First, a group of peasants secretly dug up Rakovic to check for signs of vampirism; they then reburied him. When the local priest found out, he was displeased. He led peasants back to the grave and made them dig up the body again so that he could kill the vampire. The priest poured holy water on the corpse, and the body was reburied. The vampire attacks continued. Three days later, villagers returned to the grave a third time and dug up the body. This time, they used their own remedies. They shot the corpse, cut off the head, and reburied the remains. And this time, the attacks stopped. The vampire was killed.[3]

Figure 4.2 *After the spread of Christianity, remedies such as holy water were introduced to ward off vampires.* (Scott Speakes/Corbis)

Vampires Invade New England

The vampire cult of Eastern Europe has been the center of a great deal of attention since the 1700s, but few people know that North America was the scene of a vampire wave that lasted for more than a century.

From the late 1700s to nearly the turn of the twentieth century, vampire cases rocked New England. Residents blamed deaths on vampires, and corpses were dug up, mutilated, and burned. These extreme measures were taken in desperate attempts to save the lives of sick people. Most of the deaths were caused by epidemics of tuberculosis, smallpox, and measles. Even in the eighteenth and nineteenth centuries, people had little understanding of what caused epidemics. In New England, early settlers brought with them folklore about vampires as the causes of certain kinds of deaths, especially wasting illnesses, such as cancer and tuberculosis. Thus, when highly infectious diseases like tuberculosis claimed multiple lives in a family, rumors began that vampirism was the cause.

Families dug up the bodies of spouses, sons, and daughters whose lives had been claimed by disease. They burned the corpses and made medicines with the ashes of the vital organs. The corpse medicine was fed to living persons who were sick and in danger of dying. The belief at the time was that a dose of what killed one person, which would be in the corpse, became medicine that could cure another. Imagine being extremely sick and being given a liquid medicine that contained the ashes of one of your family members! Could you drink it? Tragically, most of those who did drink corpse medicine died, anyway.

Here are some of the major vampire cases of New England, starting with the earliest on record:

RACHEL HARRIS

Rachel Harris was one of the first noted cases, occurring in 1793 in Manchester, Vermont. In 1792 Rachel married a sea captain, Isaac Burton. Her happiness was short-lived. After the wedding she fell ill with tuberculosis and died the next year. Burton remarried, but his second wife, Hulda, also contracted tuberculosis.

Word spread that a demon vampire—probably Rachel—was sucking Hulda's blood. Family and friends persuaded Burton that Hulda could be saved if the proper sacrifices were made. He ordered Rachel's body to be dug up. Her heart, liver, and lungs were cut out and burned on a blacksmith's forge, and then offered on an altar as a sacrifice to the demon vampire.

Hulda could not be saved. She died soon thereafter.

SARAH TILLINGHAST

Poor Sarah Tillinghast—after she died of tuberculosis in 1796, in South County, Rhode Island, she was blamed for the deaths of five of her 13 brothers and sisters.

The story goes that Sarah's father, Stuckley, had a premonition of disaster in a recurring dream. Stuckley farmed peaches, and in his dream, half of his harvest was withered and dead—and Sarah was present. Not long after the dreams started, Sarah sickened and died. Several members of the family, including her mother, Honour, said that Sarah was returning from the dead as a vampire to pester them at night and give them nightmares. Five of the remaining children sickened and died.

When Honour herself fell ill, Stuckley was moved to take extreme measures. All six dead children were dug up. Five were well decomposed, but Sarah's corpse was not, indicating that she had become a vampire. Stuckley cut out her heart and burned it on a rock.

One more child, Ezra, sickened and died, but Honour recovered, as did her nocturnal visits from her dead daughter and the nightmares they caused.

FREDERICK RANSOM

Frederick Ransom, of South Woodstock, Vermont, was a 20-year-old college student when tuberculosis claimed his life in 1817. His family had a superstition that people who died of tuberculosis would infect the living from the grave, a twist on vampirism. To prevent other family members from dying, Frederick's father made a traditional vampire remedy and dug up his body and had it burned on a blacksmith's forge.

It was all in vain. Frederick's mother, sister, and two brothers soon died of the same disease.

NANCY YOUNG

Nancy Young, who lived in Foster, Rhode Island, was the second of eight children. She died of tuberculosis at age 19 in 1827. Soon, other children in the Young family got sick, and Nancy was suspected of being a vampire and causing their illness.

Captain Young ordered the body of his daughter to be taken out of her grave and burned on a pyre. While the corpse burned, the Young family stood around it and inhaled the fumes. They believed that this would prevent more deaths.

They were wrong. Five more children died, all of tuberculosis.

THE RAY FAMILY

In 1845 the Henry B. Ray family of Jewett City, Connecticut, suffered its first tuberculosis loss with the death of their second oldest son.

Four years later, Henry himself died, and in 1851, another son died. The nervous family believed the two sons had become vampires, and had them dug up and burned to prevent more deaths in the family. Two more sons became ill: One survived, and one died in 1854.

ROSE FAMILY

In 1874 the William G. Rose family of Exeter, Rhode Island, lost a daughter to tuberculosis. As in the cases of Rachel Harris and Sarah Tillinghast, the dead daughter was said to return from the grave to vampirize the remaining family members. William had his daughter dug up and her heart burned to ashes in an effort to stop the attacks. It apparently worked.

There are other interesting aspects to this case. William G. Rose may have consulted later with George Brown in the famous Mercy Brown case, described below. Rose may have been influential in persuading Brown to dig up his dead family members and to have Mercy's organs burned. Also, in another interesting connection, Rose's second wife, Mary, was the great-granddaughter of Stuckley Tillinghast, the father of Sarah.

NELLIE VAUGHN

Nellie Vaughn of West Greenwich, Rhode Island, was 19 years old in 1889 when pneumonia claimed her life. She was buried in Plain Meeting House Cemetery with a tombstone that read, "I am waiting and watching for you." Her death was an unfortunate turn of fate, and no other member of her family died, nor was there any hint of a wasting illness such as might be associated with vampires. Even her tombstone message was not unusual for the times, as people hoped that their loved ones would be waiting to reunite with them in the afterlife.

Nellie might still be resting peacefully and anonymously if not for urban legend. An urban legend is a supposedly true story that starts to circulate by word of mouth, until more and more people believe it. The story is usually said to be passed on by a friend of a friend, and where it started is hard, if not impossible, to pin down.

In 1977 Nellie became swept up in an urban legend, when a local newspaper article associated her with vampires. The signs of her vampirism, according to the article, were that Nellie's grave was sunken and no vegetation would grow around it. The source of the association has never been identified, but common versions of the urban legend attribute it to a local high school teacher. Both of these signs were certain indicators of vampirism in earlier times in Europe, even though both have natural explanations. It's not unusual for dirt to shift and graves to sink in, and the presence or lack of plants could be due to many reasons.

Nonetheless, that was all it took to interest people, especially teenagers. Curiosity seekers invaded the tiny cemetery. Graves were vandalized, Nellie's tombstone was stolen, and attempts were even made to dig up her body.

By 1982 the members of the little church next to the cemetery were out of patience. Nellie's tombstone was removed to discourage thrill seekers. Yet, people still visit the cemetery today. Some say they hear a ghostly girl whisper, "I am perfectly pleasant." Even though the urban legend has been debunked, Nellie will forever remain linked to vampire lore—perhaps as the vampire girl who wasn't.

MERCY BROWN

The most famous of all New England vampire cases was the last. Mercy Brown of Exeter, Rhode Island, was 19 years old in 1892 when a tuberculosis epidemic struck her family. Her mother, Mary, and her sister, Olive, died. Then her brother, Edwin, got sick, and then Mercy got sick. She died on January 18 that year.

Meanwhile, Edwin grew worse and seemed certain to die. People went to Edwin and Mercy's father, George Brown, and convinced him that the only way to save Edwin was if he took medicine made with parts of his dead family. Brown resisted and then finally agreed. In a public event in March 1892, the graves of Mercy, Olive, and Mary were opened and their corpses were examined for signs of the vampire condition. That is, lack of decay and decomposition.

Mary was partially turned into a dry mummy. Olive was only a skeleton with a thick growth of hair remaining. But Mercy was in good condition, and she was thought to have shifted in her coffin, just like the vampires of old. A medical doctor cut out her heart and liver. Spectators were astonished to see clotted blood drip from the organs, as though they were still fresh. The organs were placed on a rock and burned to ashes. The ashes were given to Edwin. He was instructed to mix them in his medicine and drink them. Edwin did as told—but the awful remedy failed, and he soon died.

Mercy Brown's grave in Exeter is said to be haunted to this day. Visitors say they can hear a girl's voice begging for help. A ghost of a woman in white walks a path from a crypt to her grave. People report seeing a blue light or a glowing ball of light hovering over the grave, and other visitors claim they can hear a girl's voice whisper, "Please help me, let me out."

Poor Mercy was only a young woman who died too soon. The unfortunate circumstances of her death have linked her forever to vampires.

THE END TO THE SCARES

In 1882 the bacteria responsible for tuberculosis was identified. This discovery, coupled with other advances in medicine, brought an end to the belief that vampires cause infectious disease. By the early twentieth century, tuberculosis patients were placed in large sanatoriums, where doctors experimented on them with medical techniques such as surgeries, fresh air, medicines, and diet. The unlucky ones who didn't make it were turned over to their families for private burials. The disease-carrying vampire was gone.

Figure 5.1   *Doctors inject goat's blood into a woman's arm as treatment for tuberculosis in this 1891 drawing. Before the bacteria that causes the disease was discovered, many deaths from tuberculosis were blamed on vampires.* (Mary Evans Picture Library)

6

The V-Files: Stranger-Than-Strange True Vampire Cases

It is said that truth is stranger than fiction. Vampires in fiction are a strange breed, but real vampires are stranger still. Some of the vampire cases recorded throughout history are so bizarre they seem like fiction.

LAST SEEN DRIVING A LATE-MODEL COFFIN

A coffin is a container for burying the dead. It should keep the dead in their proper place: the grave. A vampire somehow manages to escape its coffin to return to the realm of the living. Various practices exist for ensuring that vampires stay put six feet under. Coffins were filled with sand, seeds, or grains, which, according to lore, vampires must count or eat particle by particle before they can escape. Heavy stones placed upon coffins before they are covered with earth also will confine restless spirits. But apparently something went awry in one particular burial. An enterprising vampire not only left his grave, but also took his coffin with him to use like an automobile, according to an oral account recorded in modern times in Romania.

The vampire was a man who had been killed in a stabbing. After his burial, he was seen driving about town in his spectral coffin. People whispered that he was looking for his wife and daughter. The dead man would get out and look around. Then he would get back in his coffin, shut the lid, and drive off back to his grave. Once he asked his former neighbors where his wife and daughter had gone. Nobody wanted the vampire to hang around, so they told him that his family had moved away. Soon, to everyone's relief, the vampire stopped coming back.[1]

That's one way to get rid of a vampire—just tell him that the victims he's looking for have moved out of town. But don't provide a forwarding address!

WANTED: UNDEAD OR ALIVE

Today, people impersonate vampires because they think it is glamorous or fun. Once upon a time, people impersonated vampires in order to stage all sorts of crimes and affairs. Vampire fraud was profitable! Criminals used the fear of the dead to their advantage.

In Europe, fake vampires put on burial shrouds and lurked about mills and granaries, especially during times of hunger. They scared away guards and employees by moaning and shrieking like vampires. When the terrified employees fled, the fake vampires helped themselves to food. Youths banded together in early versions of street gangs, dressed in burial clothes, and impersonated vampires. They vandalized villages and burglarized homes.

Even in the early part of the twentieth century, people in remote villages were still fooled by fake vampires. In one case, a gang of fake vampires went up on rooftops and threw stones at people, causing them to run from their homes. While they were gone, the men's wives and children ran into the empty homes and stole whatever they could carry away. The vampire gang moved from village to village, avoiding capture by the police and injuring many people with their stone throwing. One night an abbot decided he was going to catch them in the act. He was a fat man and with great effort climbed up on a rooftop. When the fake vampires appeared

Figure 6.1 *Vampires are somehow able to get out of their coffins and wreak havoc on the living. One vampire in Romania is said to have used his coffin as transportation!* (Daniel Smith/zefa/Corbis)

and started their stone throwing, the abbot lunged out and caught several of them. He turned them over to the local police. So ended the vampire crime spree.

More common than thievery was vampire fraud committed in the name of love. People who wanted to cover up affairs said they were being visited at night by vampires. Imagine believing that one! But it was easy to do so in earlier times, when people believed that vampires were just as interested in sex after death as they were while they were alive. If a woman became pregnant out of wedlock, she passed off the baby as the child of a vampire husband. Villagers often were too frightened to ask questions or investigate.

One clever farmer draped himself in a white shirt and white sheet to imitate burial garments. He made the rounds of villages looking for young women to romance and introduced himself as a vampire. His pick-up line worked, probably because the girls were too terrified to resist. The farmer got away with the trick for quite some time. Then one night, angry peasants chased him with guns and dogs. He was nearly killed. The scare caused him to hang up his shroud and end his career as a vampire.[2]

OFFICER, I THOUGHT IT WAS JUST MY DEAD HUSBAND

A strange and tragic case of amorous vampire fraud happened in the village of Baja, Serbia (now Hungary). A woman's husband died. Two nights after his burial, a shrouded figure in white appeared at her home. The woman, who lived with her in-laws, said that her dead husband was now a vampire and was coming back to make love with her. The vampire was completely wrapped up in his white burial shroud threaded with bells. He wore a white cap and white socks. When he appeared, ringing his bells, moaning and jerking about, the in-laws tore out of the house. Somehow the widow was brave enough to stay. The vampire spent the night, and then he left with much bell ringing, clanking, loud cries, and rattling to imitate noises associated with the walking dead. The racket was enough to keep everyone away.

These visits went on. Stories circulated around the village. It was whispered that the vampire rode people like they were donkeys. He was seen drifting about at midnight. Whenever he arrived at the widow's home, the same thing happened: everyone but the widow took off. She was a brave soul!

If the vampire visits had ended soon, probably no one would have minded in the long run. But the vampire came night after night for three months. Finally, people grew weary of being disturbed, and they got suspicious. Three young men decided they would catch this dead man.

The youths plotted with the in-laws to set a trap. Armed with heavy ropes, they hid behind the kitchen door. The vampire arrived at midnight, and, as usual, scared the in-laws out of the house. The youths jumped out and grabbed him. The vampire put up a mighty struggle, but could not escape. When the youths tore off his cap and shroud, they found that the vampire was the widow's neighbor—a man very much alive.

The youths turned him over to the authorities. The next day, the fake vampire and the widow were taken to the courthouse and questioned. On the surface, it looked like a case of an affair that started after the woman's husband died, but the case took a shocking turn. The widow and her neighbor had been attracted to each other for a long time. It was a fatal attraction. They wanted to have an affair, but they had no place to meet in secret. They poisoned the husband so that the lover could pose as the dead man coming back from the grave.

After their confession, the widow and her lover were convicted of murder and sentenced to death. The vampire was hanged and the widow was beheaded beneath the gallows.[3]

THE DIARRHEA VAMPIRES

Why hasn't Hollywood jumped on this one?

In the early eighteenth century, an epidemic of diarrhea swept through the entire population of Lastovo Island off the coast of Dubrovnik (now in Croatia). The affliction was so severe that people died. What could be responsible for the runs but vampires? It was obvious! Moreover, anyone who died at the hands of a vampire became a vampire, thus increasing the intestinal misery of the living.

The villagers took it upon themselves to open graves until they found the culprit corpse or corpses. This had to be done in strict secrecy and under the cover of darkness, for the local Christian church officials had banned vampire hunting.

Grave after grave was opened. Many corpses were normal, that is, in wretched stages of decay. The first grave opened was that of a man who had died of drowning a year earlier—a death that according to lore meant a devil would inhabit the corpse and turn it into a vampire—but his corpse had been reduced to a skeleton, and thus he was not a vampire. Three more graves were opened but revealed no vampires. As they closed the graves, the vampire hunters shouted out pleas for forgiveness from God and the dead.

Other graves were desecrated in the attempts to find the diarrhea vampires. Corpses believed to be in a vampire condition were mutilated, dismembered, and chopped up with stakes, pruning knives, stilettos, and axes. Sometimes positive identification was made of vampire corpses by the peculiar sounds they made as they were staked and cut, as well as by dog and donkey noises heard at night throughout the village.

It was inevitable that this frantic nighttime activity could not continue undetected. The church authorities rounded up some of the vampire hunters and accused them of grave desecration. The men were put on trial. After listening to long and gruesome testimonies, a court found 17 residents guilty. The men offered no defense and threw themselves on the mercy of the archbishop of Dubrovnik.

The sentences given by the archbishop called for all 17 to wear a stone about their necks and visit three churches, hear holy mass, and call out for God's mercy and forgiveness for their crimes. Some of the defendants were required to perform this sentence for two to four years. One defendant also was required to beg loudly for the forgiveness of the people. The defendants were threatened with excommunication if they failed to obey their sentences.

The record does not state what became of the diarrhea epidemic itself, but it probably, well, *ran* its course.[4]

Vlad the Bad

He was a poster bad boy for his times. He slaughtered thousands of people—his enemies, even his own people—in most unusual ways. Vlad Tepes ruled his empire with an iron fist and an iron spike. Today, one can't go anywhere in Romania without seeing his name and image. He's virtually a national hero. They call him the "historical Count Dracula." But was Vlad a vampire or just a nasty man?

SON OF THE DEVIL

Vlad Tepes, whose name means "Vlad the Impaler," was born into troubled times. His homeland was Wallachia, a province south of Transylvania, which is now part of Romania. No one knows exactly where in Wallachia he was born. The city of Sigishoara (pronounced Sig-ee-shwara) holds the honor today.

Vlad's father, Vlad II Dracul ("Vlad the Devil") came into ruling power in 1433, two years after little Vlad was born. He was a *voivode*, a prince. Wallachia was under constant threat by invading Turks, who were renowned for their ruthless fighting ways. There were constant clashes. Some were part of the Crusades and some were waged by the Turkish Ottoman empire in its campaign to expand in land and power. Vlad Dracul held his power by force. He had to be as ruthless as all of his enemies. Hence his name, "the Devil."

In 1447 Vlad II Dracul was killed. Young Vlad and his brother, Radu, fled to the enemy camp, the Ottoman court. Vlad made an alliance with the Turks. In less than a year, he invaded Wallachia with Turkish support. In 1456, he seized control. Vlad's ability to hold his power required him to be even more ruthless than his father, and he earned the name Vlad Dracula, "Vlad, son of the Devil."

REIGN OF TERROR

Vlad set up his residence in Targoviste, the capital of Wallachia. There he kept a watchful eye on any threats to his power. The Turks were always a problem. Even more problematic were the boyars, a class of noblemen who were constantly maneuvering to increase their own wealth and power. In many ways Vlad feared the boyars more than the Turks.

Vlad made certain that the boyars knew who was boss. He invited 500 of them to a feast at court, and then quizzed them on how many princes there were in Wallachia. No one gave the correct answer, seven, and so Vlad had every single one of the boyars impaled on stakes.

If he suspected anyone of treason, he had them and their families arrested and tortured. After they were broken in torture, he had them impaled on stakes. Women, men, and children alike were killed this way. Death was slow and agonizing.

Vlad had entire villages burned and their crops destroyed. He burned people, too. A group of beggars was torched because Vlad blamed them for spreading disease. He forced people to dig their own graves and then had them beheaded while they knelt by the holes. Their bodies were shoved in.

He had others boiled alive in huge pots. The pots had lids with large holes in them. The victims were forced to put their heads through the holes while their bodies cooked in the boiling water. Vlad watched their suffering. Once he boiled a major enemy and forced the man's followers to eat him.

Figure 7.1 *Vlad Tepes, also known as "Vlad the Impaler."* (Fortean Picture Library)

When a group of visiting Turk ambassadors did not remove their turbans fast enough in Vlad's court, Vlad had the turbans nailed to their heads.

Vlad is especially famous for how he got one of his castles restored. Castle Poenari, located on a cliff high above the Arges River, was in ruins by the time Vlad came to power. He liked its strategic position and decided to rebuild it—with a little help from his subjects. He invited boyars and their families to a big Easter feast. (Surely by then they were leery of Vlad's feasts, but they could not refuse a command to attend.) While the people ate and danced, he rounded up the older men and women and impaled them on stakes. The younger ones, including children, were sent off as slave labor to rebuild Castle Poenari brick by brick. People toiled up a narrow road to a point high over the Arges River. They were whipped and beaten, and worked until their clothes literally fell off their backs. Many died, falling in their tracks.

A VIOLENT END

Vlad's reign of terror lasted only six years, but it was long enough for him to murder as many as 20,000 people, according to some estimates. In 1462 the Turks attacked. Vlad managed to escape from Castle Poenari. Some say there was a secret staircase that led down to the riverbed, but no staircase has ever been found. Legend has it that Vlad's wife was stuck behind. Rather than face the brutal Turks, she flung herself over the castle walls to her death in the Arges River below.

The Turks gave the Wallachian throne to Vlad's brother, Radu. They captured Vlad and sent him to prison in Hungary, where he served 13 years. He bargained his way out in 1475, and immediately started plotting to retake the throne. Vlad was successful in 1476, but by then the Turks had had enough of him. They invaded once more and killed him.

There are different versions of Vlad's manner of death, and no one knows the real truth. He might have been killed in battle. One

Figure 7.2   *Castle Poenari.*   (Author's collection)

version holds that the Turks cut off his head and put it on a pole in Constantinople, their capital. No one knows where Vlad is buried, either. It is rumored he was buried at a monastery in Snagrove, but his grave has never been found.

THE COUNT DRACULA CONNECTION

Vlad Tepes might have faded into history as a minor, bloodthirsty prince had it not been for Bram Stoker, an Irish writer with an interest in the paranormal. Four hundred years after Vlad's bones had long

gone to dust, Stoker came upon his name and history while research-
ing a novel about a vampire, originally named Count Wampyr. He
liked the name Dracula—it had flair and power and rolled nicely off

The Blood Countess

Elizabeth Bathory was so fond of blood that she was called "the Blood Countess." Her vampirism is unique in history. The Tran-sylvanian countess was no restless dead or unholy corpse. Her thirst for blood took the form of baths, not food. Many a young maiden was sacri-ficed to her dark needs.

Born in 1560, the beautiful and wealthy countess was spoiled and mean. So mean, in fact, that she must have been mentally unstable. She was feared for her extreme cruelty to servants and peasants at Castle Savar, where she lived with her husband, Count Ferencz Nadasdy. She amused herself with sorcery.

By age 25 she thought her beauty was fading. When her husband died in 1604, she snapped. She became obsessed with regaining her lost beauty. One day an accident convinced her that blood was the ticket to youthfulness. When a maid displeased her, Bathory slashed the girl's face with a pair of scissors. Blood splashed upon Bathory's hand. It seemed to make the skin softer and younger in appearance.

Soon Bathory was bathing daily in the blood of virgins, performing a ritual given to her by her favorite sorceress, Darvulia. Bathory sent scouts into villages to recruit girls to be servants. But once in the castle, a terrible fate awaited them. They were fattened up like geese, then tortured and bled to death. Bathory bathed herself in the sprays of blood. There is no record that she ever drank blood in the traditional vampire sense. Nonetheless, she killed for blood in order to try to sustain her youthful beauty—a form of vampirism indeed.

For a time, the blood baths seemed to work a magic on Bathory's waning beauty. In 1609 Darvulia died, and Bathory became desperate the tongue. "Son of the devil" was an apt name for his evil vampire. The fictional Count Wampyr became Count Dracula. The details of that creation are told in the next chapter.

to stop the march of time. Another sorceress told her she should replace the peasant victims with girls of nobility. Bathory did so, and it finally proved to be her undoing. When young aristocrats began disappearing, Bathory's own cousin had her investigated. The evidence of her crimes was shocking. By Bathory's own account in her diary, she had vampirized more than 600 victims.

Bathory's accomplices were executed. The countess herself was never charged with any crimes, nor put on trial. Her outraged cousin, Count

Figure 7.3 *Elizabeth Bathory, or "the Blood Countess," bathed in the blood of virgins to maintain her beauty.* (Fortean Picture Library)

George Thurzo, believed her to be insane. He ordered her locked up inside her bedroom in her castle, never to be free again. Her only view of the outside world was through tiny slits in the walls. Her food was delivered through a slot in the door.

Bathory suffered in silence and isolation for five years. She died on August 21, 1614.

Besides his name Vlad contributed a little of himself to the fictional Count: his ruthlessness, his power, and his heritage as a *voivode*. There the resemblance stops. Vlad Tepes may have been bloodthirsty in the sense that he spilled a lot of blood, but there is no evidence that he ever drank blood or was ever a vampire.

Nonetheless, Romania makes the most of its most famous son. An entire Dracula tour industry promotes the Vlad-Count Dracula connection. The ruins of Castle Poenari have been restored enough to allow visitors, who must climb 1,500 steps to reach it. Every kind of merchandise you can imagine has Vlad's likeness on it.

VAMPIRES IN ROMANIA TODAY

Despite the lack of a concrete vampire connection to Vlad, there is plenty of other evidence of the vampire cult in modern-day Romania. In rural areas, the horses that draw carts and wagons often wear earlocks made of long red yarn. In folklore, red is a color that repels evil. It prevents livestock from becoming bewitched or being attacked by a vampire. Precautions are sometimes taken at burial to prevent someone from coming back as a vampire. People might stick a pin in the corpse's navel—a modern version of a stake, intended to pin a vampire into the grave.

It is not unusual for villagers to say they have vampires in their family history. Even today, if a dead person is suspected of being a vampire and making others sick, traditional remedies are taken. In 2004, for example, a dead man was dug up in a village about 100 miles from Bucharest, the capital of Romania. Since his death, three relatives had fallen mysteriously ill. His heart was cut out with a curved sickle. According to local lore, the heart made a squeaking noise, which proved the man was a vampire. The heart was placed on an iron plate and burned to ashes. The ashes were mixed in liquid, which the sick relatives drank—a little hair of the bat that bit them, so to speak.

The remedy apparently worked for the dead man's nephew—he was soon completely recovered.[1]

From Count Dracula to the Vampire Lestat and Beyond

For Bram Stoker, Whitby, England, is the perfect place to write about his fictional creation, a vampire. Remote and brooding, the little town tucked between steep hills and the rough North Sea in Yorkshire near the Scottish border has just the right macabre feel. Late at night, while brown bats wheel about the darkened town, Stoker sits in his rented rooms and toils away with pen and paper.

In his fertile imagination, Whitby itself becomes a player in Stoker's story. Here Count Dracula, the fearsome Transylvanian vampire, stages his attack on England. The town's harbor is the scene of a mysterious sailing ship crash. The *Demeter* plows to shore with all its crew dead, the corpse of the captain lashed to the wheel, and an extremely large wolf aboard that escapes into the countryside. The ruins of an abbey serve as the setting for the vampire to attack the helpless young Lucy, while her friend Mina dashes across the night landscape in a futile attempt to save her.

Whitby lights Stoker's imagination like a bonfire. The results are engraved in history, in the most famous vampire novel ever written: *Dracula*. Since *Dracula* was published in 1897, every vampire novel written—and there have been thousands of them—owes a debt to Bram Stoker.

DRACULA'S MAKER

Stoker was a man of no towering literary talent, but timing is everything. Like a lot of successful people, he had the right idea at the right time. Even so, Stoker was not graced by success during his life: It happened after he died, and his vampire lived on.

Stoker was born on November 8, 1847, in Clontarf, Ireland, and was named after his father, Abraham (Bram for short). He was a sickly child, but fortunately gained better health as he grew into adulthood. From the beginning, he was a writer, scribbling away about the fantasies in his mind.

In 1870 Stoker graduated from Trinity College in Dublin. Like most youths of the day, he followed in his father's footsteps and became a civil servant. It was a dull career for a young man with a vivid imagination. Stoker found his creative outlet in the theater. Night after night, he attended plays. He began writing reviews for the newspapers. In 1879 he published his first book, *Duties of Clerks of Petty Sessions in Ireland*, based on his civil servant duties at Dublin Castle. Bor-ing!

Stoker's involvement in the theater world soon led to a meeting that changed his life. The talented and esteemed English actor, Henry Irving, took a liking to him and hired him to be his acting manager in London. Stoker jumped at the chance. He took his bride, Florence, to England and started a new career.

Tied to the blazing star of Irving, Stoker rose in English society. He became a lawyer. He worked long and hard hours for Irving. Still, he managed to write short stories and eventually novels on the side.

Stoker was fascinated by the supernatural, and put supernatural themes and elements in some of his stories. One of them concerned a vampire, a creature that had taken public fancy by storm. In 1890 he discovered Whitby and began spending holidays in the area. Nearby was Cruden Bay, where Stoker visited the impressive ruins of Slains Castle. Stoker began work on his vampire novel in 1890, writing in London and on holiday in Whitby and Cruden Bay.

Figure 8.1   *Bram Stoker, author of* Dracula.   (Bettmann/Corbis)

Stoker had high hopes for *Dracula* when the novel was published in 1897, but the book was met with a collective yawn and mixed reviews. What was worse, Irving himself hated it. Stoker had hoped Irving would want to produce it as a play.

Irving and his theater, the Lyceum, fell on hard times. The great actor died in 1905. Strapped for money, Stoker wrote furiously for additional income. *Dracula* was not much of a success, but it managed to stay in print until Stoker's death on April 20, 1912, at age 64.

Left with a meager estate, widow Florence looked to Bram's writings to make money. She commissioned a play based on *Dracula* and sold film rights to Universal Pictures. Their film, *Dracula*, starring an unknown actor named Bela Lugosi, came out in 1931. It was a sensation and put Bram, vampires, and Count Dracula on the map. Florence lived to see the glory. She died on May 25, 1937.

Today, more than 100 years since the publication of *Dracula*, vampires have become a billion-dollar industry. Stoker would be absolutely staggered by the fame and money generated by his creation. Even though *Dracula* got off to a rocky start, the novel has never been out of print. Literary critics, historians, and fans have endlessly studied Stoker's life and his diary notes on Dracula. They want to know: What was he thinking, and when did he think it? How was Dracula born?

THE COUNT'S LITERARY ANCESTORS

Plenty of vampires had appeared in fiction and drama before Stoker ever set his pen to paper on those fateful days and nights in Whitby. He had lots of models to draw on. When the sensational news of the vampire cult spread through Europe and England in the mid-eighteenth century, artists immediately put them into poems. The first vampire story, "Wake Not the Dead," was published in German around 1800.

The first English story about vampires was "The Vampyre," published anonymously in a magazine in 1819. It was written by John Polidori, who had plagiarized an oral vampire story he heard told by

Figure 8.2   *Bela Lugosi as the title role in* Dracula *(1931).* (Author's collection)

his employer, the famous poet Lord Byron. Byron was so angry that he wrote his vampire story for publication himself to set the record straight. "The Vampyre" concerns an English aristocrat, Lord Ruthven, who becomes a vampire and seduces a young woman.

In 1847 a serial novel called *Varney the Vampire* debuted in England. It was called a "penny dreadful" because it was cheap, both in cost and quality. Varney, too, was an aristocrat gone bad. "Carmilla," a short story by J. Sheridan Le Fanu, came out in 1879. This important vampire tale centers on a young aristocratic woman who vampirizes another young woman.

From 1820 onward, the vampire was a popular figure on stage. Even a vampire opera, *Der Vampyr*, was produced in 1878. The vampire was a wonderful device: It could be used to deal with social issues, fear of death, violence, and, of course, sex, which could be disguised in the seduction of blood-taking.

Thus, Bram Stoker was only one more artist in a long line of vampire enthusiasts.

Stoker was an excellent researcher. His notes showed that he consulted 32 sources, including history, folklore, and news accounts. He found some works on Transylvanian history and culture, which is how he became acquainted with the infamous Vlad Tepes, or Vlad Dracula. Prior to discovering Vlad, Stoker had named his villain Count Wampyr, a rather wimpy name compared to Dracula. At the time, very little was known about Transylvania, and so the folklore Stoker found must have seemed exotic indeed.

Stoker never visited Romania or Transylvania himself.[1] His descriptions of the Carpathian Mountains and the Borgo Pass, where Dracula has his castle, were based on Stoker's memories of a trip he made to Switzerland. The craggy, dangerous cliffs he describes are nothing like the real Borgo Pass, which is an area of gentle, rolling green and forested countryside.

Like any storyteller, Stoker embellished and made up many things. Some of his "truths" about vampires are only fiction, yet they have been included in so many vampire books and films since then that many people today consider them fact. See the sidebar "True or False? Ten Things You Need to Know About Vampires" in Chapter 3.

THE COUNT'S SPAWN

Dracula was a huge hit on stage and on screen, and that had an impact on fiction. In the 1930s, vampires entered pulp fiction, horror, and science fiction. One of horror author Robert Bloch's most notable stories was "The Cloak," published in 1939, a comic tale about an actor who acquires a cloak worn by a real vampire, and is transformed into a fanged, bloodthirsty monster when he puts it on.

It wasn't until 1954 that another major vampire novel made the scene: *I Am Legend* by Richard Matheson. *I Am Legend* is still in print and ranks as second only to *Dracula* in enduring popularity. It was originally published as a science fiction novel, not a horror novel. The dark story features a world ravaged by a vampire plague that has either killed people or turned them into vampires. There is only one human man left on earth, who has to battle the vampires and deal with his isolation and loneliness.

I Am Legend has been made into a film three times: in 1964, as *The Last Man On Earth*, starring Vincent Price; in 1971, as *The Omega Man*, starring Charlton Heston; and in 2007, as *I Am Legend*, starring Will Smith. A graphic novel accompanied the 2007 release.

The copyright on *Dracula* expired in 1968. Authors were now free to borrow the Count. Dracula and Dracula-like figures became both villains and heroes in novel after novel. What's more, the new breed of vampire gained a conscience. Count Dracula was one-dimensional by comparison. He was driven to drink blood, like a supernatural animal. He didn't worry about the morals or ethics of it. The new vampire did. Vampires who were concerned about their victims or about their own nature were appealing to readers.

For example, Dracula becomes more human-like in Fred Saberhagen's novels, beginning with *The Dracula Tape* in 1975. Dracula expresses his thoughts and feelings, and says he is not the monster that people think he is. In *The Holmes-Dracula File* (1978), Dracula teams up with another giant of fiction, super sleuth Sherlock Holmes, created by Arthur Conan Doyle. Dracula and Holmes work together to solve serial killings in which victims are drained of blood.

Another sympathetic vampire is Saint-Germain, the hero of Chelsea Quinn Yarbro's popular novels. Saint-Germain debuted in *Hotel Transylvania* in 1978. He is based on both Dracula and the legendary historical figure Count Saint-Germain, a mysterious aristocrat and politician rumored to have discovered the secret of immortality.

Bats, Rats, and Shape-shifting

Vampires are believed to be expert shape-shifters. They take many forms—animal, human, and fantastical creature—in order to fool their prey. In other forms, they can attack more effectively and get away faster than if they are in human form.

Dracula and his fictional vampire kin are famous for shifting into the forms of huge bats. Bram Stoker, the author of *Dracula*, knew that most people have a great fear of bats. Thus, a vampire in the form of a bat would be especially terrifying.

But real vampires—those described in personal experiences and in folklore—hardly ever take the form of bats. Why? The vampire cult came from Eastern Europe, where bats are not common. Instead, people believed that vampires took the forms of animals that were familiar to them and were part of their everyday lives: cats, dogs, horses, sheep, wolves, snakes, and even birds. Would a vampire donkey seem as scary as a vampire bat? Probably not. Stoker knew what he was doing!

The vampire bat is found in Central and South America. It was named after the European vampire because it feeds on the blood of animals and sometimes humans. After the Spanish Conquistadores came home to Europe telling stories about bats that drink blood, bats began to appear more often in supernatural lore.

Rats are another creature loathed and feared by many people. In fiction, the vampire can control creatures such as rats and summon them in

In the mid-1970s vampires represented opposite extremes. On one hand were vampires like those in Stephen King's *'Salem's Lot* (1975), Count-like in their evil as they spread like a virus through a small town. On the opposite end was the new breed in Anne Rice's *Interview with the Vampire* (1976). Rice's vampires were glamorous: a race of exotic, beautiful, frozen-in-time beings who had unusual powers, wealth, and knowledge.

Figure 8.3   *The vampire bat of Central and South America feeds on the blood of animals.* (Mario Quadros/AP)

hordes. As with bats, the link between vampires and rats is more due to the creativity of writers than to real experience. Count Dracula unleashes hordes of vampire-controlled mice in a scene in *Dracula*. In *Nosferatu*, a film based on *Dracula*, the vampire sends thousands of plague-bearing rats into a city to start an epidemic.

Rice shot to best-selling fame, and the public could not get enough of her vampires. In the books that followed, she introduced many characters who grappled with big moral themes about good and evil. Rice's vampires in turn influenced romance fiction. The vampire was now a desirable date and mate, not something to be feared at all costs. In other popular fiction, such as the best-selling works of Laurell K. Hamilton, vampires joined a community of supernatural characters, including werewolves, shape-shifters, extraterrestrials, angels, and more. In addition, vampires mixed with other beings to create hybrids.

More and more, vampires blurred the line between good and evil, right and wrong. They became models for people, too, inspiring a living subculture of individuals who either believed they were born vampires, or who wanted to become vampires—somehow, somewhere.

But as popular as the new vampires are, none of them have ever surpassed the Count in popularity. Dracula has reincarnated in graphic novels and in numerous comics, such as Marvel Comics' popular *Tomb of Dracula* (1972–79), featuring a team of vampire hunters who battle the Count and other supernatural villains. The Count also appeared in some of the stories about a female vampire, Vampirella, a blood-drinking, butt-kicking superheroine who fights the forces of evil.

The Entertaining Vampire

A horror movie unlike any other has come to town. The ads in the newspapers have promised the scare of a lifetime. People pack the theater to find out if this is true. They are not disappointed. On the big screen, in black and white, they are confronted with a monster so horrible and unthinkable that people cannot look. Some faint. It's sensational.

The monster? Count Dracula. The actor? An unknown named Bela Lugosi. The year is 1931, and the film *Dracula* rockets both monster and actor to instant fame.

By today's standards, *Dracula* is tame stuff. Not enough action. Not enough blood. A vampire that could use an extreme makeover. And that Lugosi guy speaks and moves in slow motion. How could he ever catch anyone, moving like molasses?

Times change, and while the 1931 film version of Bram Stoker's novel would never get out of a studio door today, back then it was on the cutting edge of horror. The film industry was still new, and people had not been exposed to much big-screen horror of any sort. Films acted out imagination in graphic detail. *Dracula*, directed by Tod Browning and produced by Universal Pictures, influenced hundreds of vampire films yet to come. Yet it almost never got made.

THE PLAGIARIZED VAMPIRE

After Bram Stoker died in 1912, his widow, Florence, was left to make do with a small estate. She needed money. One potential source of income was the film rights to *Dracula*. Before she could sell them, someone decided to help themselves to the rights—for free.

A German film company, Prana-Film, decided to make a film version of *Dracula*. They thought that if they changed names, locations, and some plot details, they would be in the clear. The result was *Nosferatu*, a silent black-and-white film starring Max Schreck as "Graf Orlok," the vampire. Directed by F.W. Murnau, the film was released in 1922 to good reviews in Germany and Europe. Despite the good reception, Prana-Film mismanaged its money and went bankrupt. *Nosferatu* would be the only film it ever made.

Meanwhile, Florence Stoker heard of the film and was sent a copy. When she saw that her husband's novel had been plagiarized, she was furious. After a great deal of effort, she succeeded in filing a lawsuit against Prana-Film. The court ruled in her favor and awarded her 5,000 pounds, about $10,000 in today's dollars. The case was appealed, and she won the appeal, too. But getting money out of a bankrupt company was like squeezing blood out of a turnip. Florence knew she would never see a schilling. So, she pressed for all copies of the film to be destroyed. The court agreed, and supposedly the sentence was carried out. But several copies of *Nosferatu* were kept in secret, and eventually resurfaced after the copyright to the novel expired in 1968.

It's a good thing for vampire fans that *Nosferatu* survived. It has become a classic of vampire films. Schreck gives a stunning performance as the creepiest vampire of all time. He looks like a corpse fresh out of the grave, pale and thin, with long sharp talons and two front teeth that are long fangs. Schreck is still creepy, demonstrating that, sometimes, fancy special effects are not needed to fire the imagination of the viewer.

THE COUNT MAKES THE BIG TIME

After years of fighting the *Nosferatu* case, a weary Florence jealously guarded her film rights. When Universal Pictures in Hollywood knocked on her door in the late 1920s, she demanded $50,000, way above what the studio could afford. Nonetheless, the studio persisted, and eventually they struck a deal. The famous actor Lon Chaney (*Phantom of the Opera*, *London After Midnight*) was director Browning's first pick for the role of the Count, but Chaney died in 1930.

Browning then did something unthinkable for a big-ticket movie— he hired a relative unknown for the title role. Bela Lugosi was a Hungarian actor yearning for the big-time in Hollywood. He had trained as a stage actor in Europe, and in 1927 landed the role of Dracula in the Broadway play version of the novel. He had a wicked stare and an imposing, deep voice. Lugosi was so eager for Hollywood film fame that he sold himself cheap.

When Lugosi first played Dracula onstage, he spoke no English, and he learned his lines one by one, phonetically, without understanding the words. He had to speak his lines slowly, and with a heavy accent. Although by the time he appeared in the movie version, he had learned English, he still had a heavy accent. Fortunately, it fit the character of the foreign, hypnotic vampire. For decades, vampire actors imitated Lugosi.

Browning stuck fairly close to the stage version of the novel, which had been written by Hamilton Deane and John L. Balderston. One curious addition were armadillos that scurried about the count's castle. Armadillos are not native to Europe and are never mentioned in the book. Perhaps Browning thought they looked strange and exotic and contributed to the spooky castle atmosphere. The film Dracula was a classy dresser, running around England in formal clothing. Polite society in Stoker's day did dress more formally than people today, but Dracula's wardrobe did get a boost for stage and screen: cape, top hat, walking stick, and so forth.

Dracula was a huge success, earning the studio $1.2 million world-wide. Lugosi was in demand. But having sold himself cheap the first time, he was never able to command a big star's salary. A year after the release of *Dracula*, he was bankrupt. Although he played vampires in other movies, he played Dracula on film only once more, in *Abbott and Costello Meet Frankenstein*, and died a poor drug addict in 1956, in the middle of filming *Plan 9 from Outer Space*.

THE NEW COUNTS

Vampires became the rage in horror films, along with werewolves and other monsters. In the 1950s a new Count took the silver screen by storm: Christopher Lee. The tall and imposing English actor broke into films in the 1950s. Meanwhile, an English film studio named Hammer Films, founded in the 1930s, was becoming *the* name in horror films. Their formula was simple: make it bloody and sexy. It worked very well.

Hammer purchased the rights to remake *Dracula*. Lee's career as the Count was launched in 1958 in *Dracula* (titled *Horror of Dracula* in the U.S. release). Lee was a major influence in the screen transition of vampire from villain to glamour guy. His vampire was thoroughly evil but also charismatic and alluring. He had sex appeal. Lee could sweep about in his Count cape far better than Lugosi. He played the Count in seven Hammer Films, often paired opposite Peter Cushing as the vampire hunter, Abraham Van Helsing.

Lee was not the only glamorous vampire. Numerous other ac-tors played Dracula, bringing varying degrees of evil and glamour to the screen. Among the most romantic counts were Frank Langella, in John Badham's 1979 *Dracula*, and Gary Oldman in Francis Ford Coppola's 1991 *Bram Stoker's Dracula*. But the vampire who best com-bines evil and appeal is not Count Dracula at all, but an entire new breed of vampire, represented by Anne Rice's Lestat. When Tom Cruise was picked for the film role, Rice reportedly did not approve. She did not think he had the right touch for evil. Cruise, however, pulled off the aristocratic, lace-wearing vampire in style, and Rice changed her mind.

In other films, vampires have developed in the opposite direction of sexy glamour—they are monsters, such as the demonic creatures in *From Dusk Till Dawn*, starring George Clooney as a robber and vampire killer. They are nasty killers, as in the Blade films, starring Wesley Snipes as Marvel Comics' super vampire hunter with a formidable weapon. Or they are dark and Gothic, like the tough vampires in *Underworld* (2003), who are at war with lycans (werewolves).

DARK SHADOWS: VAMPIRES HIT THE SMALL SCREEN

Televisions came into common use in homes in the 1950s, and people were riveted by entertainment in their living rooms. Vampires moved right in. The first famous television vampire was introduced in a soap opera—as an afterthought.

In 1966 a daytime soap opera called *Dark Shadows* made its debut on television with high hopes of being a hit. Instead, it failed. In a desperate move to save the show, a vampire was added to the cast. The rest of the story is fictional vampire history.

Dark Shadows was created by Dan Curtis, a talented man with a fondness for the paranormal. One night in 1965, Curtis had a dream in which he saw a beautiful young woman riding a train. Her destination was a dark and gloomy mansion. The dream was so vivid that Curtis could not forget it. As he thought about the dream over and over, he got the idea for a television show: a Gothic story about the tortured, wealthy Collins family in New England who live in a dark, mysterious mansion. The family hires a young woman to become a nanny. She is horrified to become part of their twisted lives.

While the idea sounded great, television audiences were not so enthusiastic. *Dark Shadows* limped along for months. By spring of

1967, it was in danger of being canceled. Curtis and his team brainstormed to save the show. Vampires were a hit in the movie theaters, so why not introduce a vampire to the plot? They had nothing to lose.

A Canadian actor named Jonathan Frid, who was unknown to American television audiences, was hired to play the role of Barnabas Collins, the family vampire. According to the story line, Barnabas was cursed by a witch to become a vampire and for 200 years had slept locked in a coffin in a family crypt. A caretaker accidentally lets him loose.

Frid had to be persuaded to take the role, for he was a stage actor. He thought he would be in several episodes and then would return to stage acting. Barnabas was an overnight sensation and sent *Dark Shadows* to the top of the television hit list. The life and career of Frid were changed forever.

In the beginning, Barnabas is evil and sinister. He attacks people and drinks their blood. But over the course of time, Barnabas becomes more sympathetic. He tries to find a cure for his blood thirst. He seeks to avoid killing people. He tries to help them rather than hurt them. Over time, Barnabas transforms from villain to hero. He is one of the first entertainment vampires to be liked rather than feared.

Dark Shadows went into deep, paranormal territory. Another Collins relative, Quentin, became a werewolf. Story lines explored curses, magic, time travel, ghosts, reincarnation, and parallel universes.

Dark Shadows lasted until 1971, with 1,225 episodes. It still has a large international fan following. It inspired many other films and television shows, including *Buffy the Vampire Slayer.*

Dark Shadows has earned a permanent cult following—but fans love the original, not remakes. In 1991 Curtis produced a new *Dark Shadows* with a new cast and new twists on the story line. Ben Cross played Barnabas. The show failed in ratings. Another attempt to resurrect *Dark Shadows* in 2003 never got out of the gate. Perhaps there can be only one Barnabas!

THE VAMPIRE KNIGHT IN SHINING ARMOR

Nick Knight is a vampire turned good guy in *Forever Knight*, a Canadian series that had a rocky history in the early 1990s. Knight became a vampire in the thirteenth century but repented his bloodthirsty ways. In modern Toronto, he works as a homicide detective, trying to make amends and regain his mortality. Rick Springfield played the title role in a pilot television movie in 1989, followed by

Paving the Way for Buffy

Before *Buffy*, there were two important films that mixed teenagers and vampires: *Fright Night* (1985) and *The Lost Boys* (1987). In both films, adults take a backseat role to the teens, who grow up in a hurry and learn on their own how to conquer evil.

In *Fright Night*, Charley, a nice boy (William Ragsdale) discovers his new next-door neighbor is a vampire. No one believes him, not even his adult role model, a television actor and horror show host (Roddy McDowall). It's up to Charley to destroy the vampire, and in the end he gets some supporting help from the actor. *Fright Night* was followed by a sequel in 1988, *Fright Night 2*, in which the horror show host redeems himself in a more dramatic way and destroys the new vampire threat.

The Lost Boys, the first major film role for Kiefer Sutherland, features alienated teens who are a rogue gang of young vampires. Outsiders with fangs, they ride motorcycles, make trouble, and flaunt adult authority. They are brought down by other teens who become vampire hunters.

Like *Buffy*, the central teens in *Fright Night* and *The Lost Boys* come from single-parent families—they have single moms who are distracted with jobs and are not in a position to solve the teens' vampire problems for them.

Geraint Wyn Davies in the series in 1992. *Forever Knight* continued the blurring of the vampire's identity as evil monster or good guy—or both.

SLAY THOSE VAMPIRES!

The most popular television show of all about vampires didn't even star a vampire. Instead, the star was a vampire killer—and a girl. *Buffy the Vampire Slayer* created a whole new universe of vampires, angels, demons, and more.

Buffy began life in 1992 as a modest, campy film. Creator and producer Joss Whedon introduced Buffy as "the One Girl, the Chosen One of each generation," who inherits the ability to slay vampires and fight the forces of darkness. In her current incarnation, Buffy is a blonde, high school cheerleader who has to balance her interest in boys and other teen things with her grave responsibility concerning good and evil.

The film, starring Kristy Swanson as Buffy and Rutger Hauer as the vampire Lothos, received little attention. But Whedon expanded his creation and improved the characters in his television version, which debuted in 1997. Starring Sarah Michelle Gellar as Buffy, the show was a super hit.

Buffy lives in a strange universe. Her high school in the small California town of Sunnyvale is full of paranormal surprises. Demonic forces are everywhere. Buffy is a reluctant slayer, but gets called to duty over and over again to fight evil. She is guided by an adult mentor, Giles, a Watcher who is assigned by the powers to help Buffy. She is helped by her friends Willow and Xander. The four of them are the "Scooby Gang," a group of paranormal do-gooders informally named after the characters in Scooby Doo cartoons.

Buffy tries to live a normal teenaged life while killing monsters, demons, shape-shifters, and evildoers and "dusting" vampires, that is, turning them into dust. It's not easy. Like many girls, she wants a romance with a boy, but the one who pursues her is a vampire named Angel. She has to deal with evil witches and a nasty vampire named Spike who has killed Vampire Slayers who came before Buffy.

Figure 9.1   *The cast of TV's* Buffy the Vampire Slayer. (Author's collection)

As the show progressed, Buffy graduates from high school, works as a waitress, and enrolls in Sunnydale University. Her supernatural warfare gets more complicated, and she deals with big issues of life and death. She even has encounters with the legendary Count Dracula, a handsome vampire who manages to feed on Buffy's blood. He offers to make her immortal but she refuses.

Buffy lasted for seven seasons. In the end Buffy returns to her old high school, Sunnydale, to be a guidance counselor. Her mother has

Girls Makes Good Vampires, Too

Most leading vampires of film and fiction are male—but don't overlook the women. Some of the deadliest vampires have been females. In folklore, anyone of either gender, or any age, can be a vampire. Some of the most famous female vampires, real and fictional, are:

- **Elizabeth Bathory**. A real-life woman and technically not a vampire, she's often included in the category because of her fondness for bathing in blood. She killed 600 young girls for their blood. The actress Ingrid Pitt portrays a Bathory-like figure in *Countess Dracula* (1971).

- **Carmilla**. She is the villain in Sheridan Le Fanu's 1879 short story by the same name. According to the story, Carmilla was the Countess Mircalla Karnstein of Europe. She quietly vampirized her victims for 150 years before being unmasked and destroyed by beheading as she lay in her bloody grave. Actress Annette Vadim portrays her in the film *Blood and Roses* (1960).

- **Lucy Westenra**. Lucy is Count Dracula's main victim in Bram Stoker's *Dracula*. Once she's one of the undead, she leaves her tomb to prey on little children. The men in the novel band together and destroy her by staking. Any Dracula film, of course, must include Lucy.

died. There is a whole new crop of Slayers, called Potentials. Demons are plotting to kill them so that the Hellmouth can open to allow more forces of evil to enter the world. In the battles, Buffy realizes that she does not have to fight evil alone, because she is one of many. The Hellmouth opens and swallows up most of Sunnydale. Buffy and some of the survivors get away on a bus, and Spike goes back to hell.

The success of *Buffy* led to fan conferences, fan fiction, and a cult following. Why was it so popular? The show was well-written and

- **Akasha.** Anne Rice's queen of the vampires stars in Rice's third vampire novel, *The Queen of the Damned* (1988). Akasha and her mate, Enkil, are a sort of Adam and Eve of the vampire race. Akasha plots to destroy nearly all the males on the planet, but Lestat foils her plan and she meets her doom. The actress/singer Aaliyah plays Akasha in the film *Queen of the Damned* (2002). Tragically, she died in a plane crash during the shooting, and the film had to be completed without her.

Figure 9.2 *Aaliyah as Akasha in* Queen of the Damned *(2002).* (Author's collection)

funny, but it involved serious issues that young people face every day in the ordinary world: fitting in with one's peers, doing well in school, dealing with adults, and making choices about right and wrong.

Buffy continues on even though the show is over. Joss Whedon and Georges Jeanty created an "eighth season" in comic book form in 2007.

In the end, it's all about good storytelling and interesting characters. *Buffy* is an example of the never-ending fascination people have with vampires and the supernatural.

IT WAS INEVITABLE: REALITY TV

Sooner or later, vampires had to hit reality television shows. Reality TV has touched just about every aspect of real life and fantasy life. In 2004 the Sci Fi Channel created *Mad, Mad House*. "Normal" people have to go and live with a house full of "Alts," or people living weird, alternative lifestyles. The Alts included a vampire, a Voodoo priestess, a witch, a naturist (clothing optional), and a "modern primitive" who wore a lot of body art. The show had eight episodes. *Mad, Mad House* was a real-life version of two fictional "alt" families that were popular on television in sitcoms from 1964–1966: *The Addams Family* and *The Munsters.*

JUST REGULAR GUYS AND GIRLS

The vampire has become a regular character on both the big and little screens, and, increasingly, in video games. *Masquerade, Buffy,* and other vampire **clans** and cultures offer players the chance to become the characters, rather than just reading about or watching them. Gaming vampires are the new breed: exotic, cunning, and supernaturally powerful, light years beyond the rotting corpses that inspired their creation.

Sometimes the good guy (or girl), and sometimes the bad, the vampire seems to have an unending appeal. Will audiences ever tire of vampires? More than 200 years after vampires joined the performing arts, popular fascination with them shows no signs of slowing down.

The Vampire Underground

They like to dress in black and especially Goth styles. They go out at night—to clubs. They may have fangs—courtesy of their dentist. Got blood? Most of them never touch the stuff. And yet they call themselves vampires.

Welcome to the vampire underground, where real people live as vampires, or at least how they think vampires should live. They are mysterious. They have their own society. They feel they have power. And many feel superior to "mere mortals." In their view, mortals just exist. Vampires, who possess the "**dark gift**," live "the Life," which is better. They are, after all, "**the Chosen**."

The previous chapters have looked at vampires from the grave. There's nothing appealing about them. Even the traditions of living vampires, people who have witchy, magical dark powers, are not a model to imitate. So who are these "real" vampires who act so cool, and how did they become what they are?

THE ENERGY VAMPIRES

Meet Lady Moira. That's not her real name, but her vampire name. She adopted it after she "awakened." Lady Moira was interested in horror films and vampires at an early age. As she grew older, she suffered from depression and often felt tired for no obvious reason.

Then one day she spent time with a girl who seemed full of energy. She wished she could feel like that. Something strange happened. She began to feel better and more energized. She noticed that the other girl's energy started to drop. As Lady Moira felt better, the girl felt worse. Finally, the girl complained of feeling exhausted and said she had to go home. Lady Moira had discovered that she was an energy vampire. She had **awakened** to her true self.

She tried experiments to deliberately suck off other people's energy. It worked. Over time and with practice, she found she could take someone's energy quickly and walk away, feeling much better herself. Sometimes the other person didn't even know what hit them.

Eventually Lady Moira found other people like her. They were vampires. She entered their secret life. There she found a whole new race of people who lived by their own laws, codes, history, and organization. As a **fledgling**, she was initiated and taught the vampire ways by a **maker**, sometimes called a **sire**.

Many of Lady Moira's fellow vampires look like ordinary people. You could walk by them on the street and never know they were different. Others look more obvious in the way they dress and act. They resemble vampires seen in films. They all have one thing in common: They need to feed off living things in order to sustain themselves. But they don't take blood—they take energy.

Energy vampires say they are born that way. They don't have enough of their own natural energy, and so they must use other people like batteries. When energy vampires awaken, they realize they just "know" how to take energy. They practice and get very good at it. They find willing partners to drain, and they sometimes take energy from others, including strangers.

THE SANGUINARIANS

Meet Lord Valerian. He is a different kind of vampire—a blood drinker, a *sanguinarian*. Lord Valerian realized when he was a child that he was fascinated by blood. He had an accident in which he cut himself with a kitchen knife. Instinctively, he sucked the cut. The blood tasted good.

Like Lady Moira, Lord Valerian awakened when he was older. He found Goth clubs and hung out with people who shared his interests in music and clothing. He met a man who told him that he was a vampire and drank blood. Lord Valerian realized then that he was a vampire, too—not just someone who was acting like a vampire but a *real* vampire. His new friend introduced him to other real vampires. They had their own secret life with their own rules and organization. Like Lady Moira, Lord Valerian was tutored by a sire. He learned how to participate in rituals of blood exchanges.

Blood-drinking vampires are not like the vampires of folklore or fiction. They do not bite people on the neck and drink all their blood. They know that too much blood will make them sick, even though blood is full of the life force. They usually take blood in very small amounts, from shallow cuts, scratches, and piercings on parts of the body that bleed easily. They call it blood play or blood sports.

Sanguinarians have willing donors (known as **black swans)**; they do not prowl around the streets looking to ambush someone like Anne Rice's vampire Lestat. Because of the dangers of blood-borne diseases such as AIDS and hepatitis, most of them screen their donors carefully. Some sanguinarians substitute other drinks for blood at times.

Like the energy vampires, sanguinarians say they are born as vampires, not "made."

THE NEW VAMPIRE

Both energy vampires and blood-drinking vampires are new, modern types of vampires who make up an underground culture. Many of these vampires believe that their kind has always existed, and that vampire bloodlines have been inherited through the ages. You have to be born a vampire, they say. You either are or you aren't. You can't be "made" or "turned" like the vampires in fiction. Those whoe pretend otherwise are only **vampabees**, vampire wannabees.

The new vampires are not dead or walking corpses. They are very much alive.

Actually, it was fiction that inspired much of the new vampire movement. As the vampire became more and more romantic and glamorous in novels and in films, instead of being feared, the vampire

It's A Vampire Empire Out There

Not everyone who likes vampires wants to live as one in an underground clan. Most vampire fans just want to appreciate vampires in entertainment and pop culture. Lots of clubs and organizations exist to serve those interests. The biggest is the international Vampire Empire.

The Vampire Empire started out as the Count Dracula Fan Club. It was founded in New York City in 1965 by Jeanne Keyes Youngson, who became interested in vampires after taking a trip to Romania. She was involved in the film industry. As the club attracted members, Youngson published newsletters and booklets about vampires in history, folklore, film, and fiction.

Youngson collected vampire memorabilia and soon had the world's largest vampire museum. In 1999 she sold most of her collection to European investors. By 2000 the club had expanded to include other subjects besides vampires, and Youngson changed the name to Vampire Empire.

The Vampire Information Network, founded in 1978 by Eric Held of Brooklyn, New York, is a place where vampire fans can correspond and get networking information.

Bernard Davies and Bruce Wightman founded the Dracula Society in London, England, in 1973. It is similar to the Vampire Empire in interests and holds meetings and organizes field trips. The society's motto is "Credo Quia Impossible," which is Latin for "I believe because it is impossible."

was idolized. Other major influences were the Goth club scene and the popularity of role-playing games, such as *Vampire: The Masquerade*.

The most influential fictional vampires were those created by Rice in her Vampire Chronicles. Lestat and his fellow blood drinkers inspired a wave of real-life imitation. The new vampires created their own secret clubs, or **havens**, with their secret passwords, jewelry, and signs. They banded together in groups, which became clans, **safehouses**, families, **courts**, **guilds**, and **covens**, governed by elders. They developed their own codes of behavior, their own sacred texts, and their own histories and mythologies. Some of them have used the spelling "**vampyre**" to distinguish themselves from the vampires of folklore, film, and fiction. Sometimes they are called HLVs, for "**human living vampires.**"

The Goth music and club scene contributed to the vampire movement, providing places where vampires could gather and meet. One person who enjoyed the club life was Father Todd Sebastian, who began organizing vampires into groups. His vision was a Vampire Nation inspired by the Rice books—a race of vampires living in their own shadowy community, co-existing with mortals. Father Todd founded the Sanguinarium in the 1990s, primarily for blood drinkers. The organization also includes energy vampires.

In 1991 the role-playing game *Vampire: The Masquerade* was published and became an instant hit. Through the game, and other role-playing games, people who were fascinated by vampires could act out their fantasies. Some of them carried the role-playing into their lives and became "vampire lifestylers," people who want to be vampires and behave and dress accordingly.

The new vampire movement expanded in the 1980s and 1990s. Vampire groups spread around the world, mostly in Western countries where vampire films and fiction are popular. In 1997 Father Todd and Michelle Belanger, an energy vampire, created **The Black Veil**, a voluntary code of ethics, etiquette, and ideals for the vampire community. The code urges common sense, respect, and responsibility for those who wish to live as vampires.

Figure 10.1 *Two modern vampires at a goth/vampire club in Manhattan.* (Mark Peterson/Corbis)

In surveys taken among vampires on both sides of the Atlantic, many vampires say they share some, but not all, characteristics with fictional vampires. Most say they are sensitive to sunlight or avoid it as much as possible. Some say they are allergic to garlic. Nearly half of them wear fake fangs, at least part of the time. Most fake fangs can be taken in and out. Some vampires pay a great deal of money to have permanent fangs capped onto their canine teeth. However, it is hard to eat normally with fangs. The human mouth is built to chew, not cut and tear.

Many vampires say that they have some psychic or supernatural powers, like fictional vampires. They don't pretend to have supernormal strength or to be able to move like lightning. Some of them do have unusual natural psychic abilities, or they learn how to develop psychic ability as part of their identity as a vampire. Those abilities might include clairvoyance, being able to see the unknown, including auras and spirits; precognition, being able to see the future; mediumship, the ability to communicate with the dead and spirits; and the ability to travel out of the body. Some, especially the energy vampires, say they can manipulate and influence the thoughts and feelings of others. In *Dracula* and many other vampire novels, the vampire has hypnotic power over people, which would be like using psychic ability to influence thoughts. Most new vampires say they do not consider themselves to be immortal, like the fictional vampire. They will die like mortals. Their immortality, they say, comes through continual reincarnation as vampires.

The vampire underground is creative. There is a constantly changing scene of vampire zines, blogs, message boards, and Web sites, music, literature, and art. Vampires have many ways of networking and staying in touch with each other.

THE FUTURE OF REAL VAMPIRES

Today's vampires may have been inspired by fiction, but they have created a very real underground culture. If the underground lasts long enough, it may become a part of the history of vampire lore. People in the future may study today's vampires as we today study the folklore and cases of centuries past.

Could a new race of "vampire people" be created? It's an intriguing idea that has been explored in fiction—and has some genuine possibilities. If there are genetic factors for such traits as natural psychic ability, allergies to garlic, a preference for nighttime hours, and so on, then if vampires marry and have children, they might pass on those traits. Over time, such "vampire" traits could become more noticeable. That would fulfill the vampires' belief that to be a vampire, you indeed have to be born as one.

Timeline

ANCIENT TIMES   People all over the world develop their beliefs about the returning dead—and ways to deal with them

1100s   William of Newburgh, an English canon, includes accounts of bloodthirsty ghosts, or revenants, in his history of England, but the term "vampire" had not been invented yet

1431   Vlad Tepes, also known as Vlad Dracula, is born in Romania, probably in Sigishoara

1476   Vlad Tepes is killed by Turks and is buried in an unknown grave

1560   Elizabeth Bathory, the "blood Countess," is born in Ecsed, Transylvania

1600s   The word "vampire" first appears in French accounts of European vampires

1614   Elizabeth Bathory dies imprisoned in a castle as punishment for her vampire blood crimes

1742   Johann Fluckinger's military report on Eastern European vampires ignites Western curiosity

1746   Augustus Dom Calmet publishes his two-volume work on ghosts and vampires in French, titled in English in 1759 *The Phantom World*

1819   "The Vampyre," a short story plagiarizing Lord Byron, is published in an English magazine

1840s   A "penny dreadful" serial novel called *Varney the Vampire* is popular in England

1872   J. Sheridan Le Fanu's important short story about a female vampire, "Carmilla," is published

1897   Bram Stoker's novel, *Dracula*, is published

1912   Bram Stoker dies, without ever seeing *Dracula* a hit

1922   *Nosferatu*, a film plagiarism of *Dracula*, is released in Europe

1931   Bela Lugosi stars in *Dracula*, based on Stoker's book

1956   Bela Lugosi dies and is buried in Los Angeles in one of his Dracula capes

1958   Christopher Lee stars in his first role as the Count in Hammer Films' *Dracula* (titled *Horror of Dracula* in the U.S.)

1960s   Vampire fan clubs form around the world

1964–1966   Vampires are in the family tree in the television sitcoms *The Addams Family* and *The Munsters*

1965   Count Dracula Fan Club is formed by Jeanne Keyes Youngson

1966   *Dark Shadows* debuts on television

1967   Barnabas Collins becomes the vampire of *Dark Shadows*

1970s   Vampire subculture groups form

1971   *Dark Shadows* ends

1973   The Dracula Society is formed in England for film and literature buffs

1976   Anne Rice's *Interview With the Vampire* is published

1991   Director Francis Ford Coppola remakes *Dracula* in *Bram Stoker's Dracula*, changing the plot to more of a reincarnation love story

1991   *Vampire: The Masquerade* role-playing game is published, influencing the vampire subculture

1992   The film *Buffy the Vampire Slayer* opens in theaters

1997   *Buffy the Vampire Slayer* becomes a hit television show

1997   The Black Veil code of ethics is created for vampire communities by Father Todd Sebastian and Michelle Belanger

2000   Count Dracula Fan Club is renamed the Vampire Empire

2003   *Buffy the Vampire Slayer* television series ends

Glossary

AWAKENED The realization a person has that he or she is a vampire, which may take more than one lifetime to fully accomplish, according to modern vampire lore

BLACK SWANS People who serve as voluntary blood donors for sanguinarians

BLACK VEIL A code of ethics and etiquette for modern living vampires who are members of the Sanguinarium, an American-based organization

CHOSEN, THE Term used by some modern living vampires to describe themselves

CLANS Social communites of modern living vampires

COURT An organization of modern living vampires

COVENS Groups or families of modern living vampires

DARK GIFT Term originally from fiction that refers to being a vampire, whether given from a vampire to a mortal, usually by mutual blood drinking, thus turning that person into another vampire, or referring to psychic and other supernatural powers

ELDERS Modern living vampires who lead or guide a clan, and serve as maker or sire to fledgling vampires

EVIL EYE A magical ability to harm others by looking at them strangely

FEEDING Eating for a modern living vampire, either by drawing off psychic energy or drinking blood

FLEDGLING In modern vampirism, a newly awakened or "made" vampire

GUILD A sub-organization within a vampire community

HAVENS   Places or establishments where modern living vampires gather in secret

HUMAN LIVING VAMPIRE (HLV)   A person who believes himself or herself to be a vampire

MAKER   The guide or master of a fledgling, who functions like an advisor or parent

NOSFERATU   Term of uncertain origins applied to vampires and the undead, popularized in Bram Stoker's novel, *Dracula*

PSI VAMPIRES (ALSO PSYCHIC VAMPIRES)   Modern vampires who draw energy off people rather than drink their blood

REVENANTS   Old term for ghosts, especially used to describe the restless dead

SAFEHOUSES   Clubs, like a bar or nightclub, where modern living vampires can be themselves

SANGUINARIAN **(ALSO SANGUINE)**   A modern vampire who drinks blood

SIRE   The guide or master of a fledgling

UNDEAD   A person who dies and does not go into the afterlife properly or stay in the grave, but escapes to attack the living as a vampire

VAMPABEES   People who want to become vampires, like wannabees

VAMPIRE   A restless ghost, a spirit, or a living person who has the ability to drain the vital life force from anything living; in folklore most often associated with the restless dead who drink the blood of the living

VAMPIRE LIFESTYLERS   People who want to become vampires like those in fiction and film, or who live like vampires according to descriptions in fiction and film

VAMPYRE   Spelling preferred by some living vampires to distinguish themselves from fictional or folklore vampires

VRESKET   Croatian word for the sound vampires make when they are staked, created by air rushing through the windpipe

Endnotes

CHAPTER 1

1. Katherine M. Wilson, "The History of the Word Vampire," in *The Vampire: A Casebook*, Alan Dundes., ed. (Madison, Wisc.: University of Wisconsin Press, 1998), p. 4.

2. Jan L. Perkowski, *The Darkling: A Treatise on Slavic Vampirism* (Columbus, Ohio: Slavica Publishers, 1989), pp. 29–230.

CHAPTER 2

1. Montague Summers, *The Vampire in Europe* (New York: E.P. Dutton & Co., 1929), pp. 136–143.

2. Paul Barber, *Vampires, Burial and Death* (New Haven: Yale University, 1988), pp. 10-13.

3. Ibid., pp. 15-18.

CHAPTER 3

1. Rosemary Ellen Guiley with J.B. Macabre, *The Complete Vampire Companion* (New York: Macmillan, 1994), p. 18.

2. Perkowski, *Op. cit.*, p. 105.

3. Jan L. Perkowski, *The Vampire of the Slavs* (Cambridge, Mass: Slavica Publishers, 1976).

CHAPTER 4

1. Rosemary Ellen Guiley, *The Encyclopedia of Vampires, Werewolves, and*
Other Monsters (New York: Facts On File, 2005), pp. 101–102.

2. Barber, *Op. cit.*, pp. 66–81.

3. John V. A. Fine, Jr., "In Defense of the Vampire," in *The Vampire: A Casebook*, *Op. cit.*, pp. 57–66.

CHAPTER 6

1. Henry A. Senn, *Were-Wolf and Vampire in Romania* (Boulder, Colo.: Eastern European Monographs, 1982), p. 8.

2. Guiley, *The Encyclopedia of Vampires, Werewolves, and Other Monsters*, *Op. cit.*, p. 294.

3. Ibid.

4. Perkowski, *Op. cit.*, pp. 85–100.

CHAPTER 7

1. "For Romanians, slaying vampires is in the blood." *Duluth News-Tribune*, March 28, 2004, pp. 1A and 9A.

CHAPTER 8

1. Elizabeth Miller, *Dracula: Sense and Nonsense* (Westcliff-On-Sea, England: Desert Island Books Ltd., 2000), p. 148.

Bibliography

Barber, Paul. *Vampires, Burial and Death: Folklore and Reality*. New Haven, Conn.: Yale University Press, 1988.

Belanger, Michelle. *The Psychic Vampire Codex: A Manual of Magick and Energy Work*. York Beach, Me.: Weiser Books, 2004.

Belford, Barbara. *Bram Stoker: A Biography of the Author of Dracula*. New York: Alfred A. Knopf, 1996.

Bell, Michael E. *Food for the Dead: On the Trail of New England's Vampires*. New York: Carroll & Graf Publishers, 2001.

Calmet, Dom Augustin. *The Phantom World: Concerning Apparitions and Vampires*. Ware, England: Wordsworth Editions in association with The Folklore Society, 2001.

Dresser, Norine. *American Vampires: Fans, Victims, Practitioners*. New York: W.W. Norton & Co., 1989.

Florescu, Radu R., and Raymond T. McNally. *Dracula: Prince of Many Faces: His Life and Times*. Boston: Little, Brown and Co., 1989.

Frayling, Christopher. *Vampyres: Lord Byron to Count Dracula*. London: Faber and Faber, 1991.

Guiley, Rosemary Ellen. *The Encyclopedia of Vampires, Werewolves, and Other Monsters*. New York: Facts On File, 2005.

Guinn, Jeff with Andy Grieser. *Something in the Blood: The Underground World of Today's Vampires*. Arlington, Tex.: The Summit Publishing Group, 1996.

Lee, Christopher. *Tall, Dark and Gruesome: An Autobiography*. London: W.H. Allen, 1977. Rev. ed. London: Victor Gollancz, 1997.

McNally, Raymond T. *Dracula Was A Woman: In Search of the Blood Countess of Transylvania*. New York: McGraw-Hill, 1983.

Miller, Elizabeth. *Dracula: Sense and Nonsense.* Westcliff-on-Sea, England: Desert Island Books, 2000.

Perkowski, Jan L. *The Darkling: A Treatise on Slavic Vampirism.* Columbus, Ohio: Slavica Publishers, 1989.

Ramsland, Katherine. *Piercing the Darkness: Undercover with Vampires in America Today.* New York: HarperPrism, 1998.

Riccardo, Martin V. *Liquid Dreams of Vampires.* St. Paul, Minn.: Llewellyn Books, 1996.

Rice, Anne. *Interview with the Vampire.* New York: Alfred A. Knopf, 1976.

Russo, Arlene. *Vampire Nation.* London: John Blake, 2005.

Silver, Alain, and James Ursini. *The Vampire Film: From* Nosferatu *to* Interview with the Vampire, 3d ed. New York: Limelight Editions, 1997.

Skal, David J. *Hollywood Gothic: The Tangled Web of* Dracula *from Novel to Stage to Screen.* New York: W.W. Norton & Company, 1990.

Stoker, Bram. *Dracula.* New York: Grosset & Dunlap, 1931.

Summers, Montague. *The Vampire in Europe.* New York: E.P. Dutton and Co., 1929.

Further Resources

The following are a few of the many Web sites devoted to vampires. All of these in turn have many links that will take you deeper into vampire territory. Vampire Clubs and Connections and Vampire Realms of Darkness are especially comprehensive.

Anne Rice
http://www.annerice.com

Buffyology: The Academic Study of Buffy
http://www.geocities.com/buffyology/

The Dracula Society
http://www.thedraculasociety.org.uk/

SD Vampire Connexion
http://www.simplydark.com/vampire.html

Vampire Clubs and Connections
http://www.geocities.com/Athens/forum/2853/clubs.htm
The granddaddy of lists! Fan clubs, societies, author fan clubs, television show fan clubs, periodicals, and more.

The Vampire Empire
http://www.benecke.com/vampire.html

Vampire Realms of Darkness
http://www.vampires.nu/pages/Organizations.cfm/PageID/16
Another comprehensive list of all kinds of vampire-related organizations.

Vampire Studies
http://www.answers.com/topic/vampire-studies

Index

Page numbers in *italics* indicate photographs.

About the Author and Consulting Editor

ROSEMARY ELLEN GUILEY is one of the foremost authorities on the paranormal. Psychic experiences in childhood led to her lifelong study and research of paranormal mysteries. A journalist by training, she has worked full time in the paranormal since 1983, as an author, presenter, and investigator. She has written 31 nonfiction books on paranormal topics, translated into 13 languages, and hundreds of articles. She has experienced many of the phenomena she has researched. She has appeared on numerous television, documentary, and radio shows. She is also a member of the League of Paranormal Gentlemen for Spooked TV Productions, a columnist for *TAPS Paramagazine*, a consulting editor for *FATE* magazine, and writer for the "Paranormal Insider" blog. Ms. Guiley's books include *The Encyclopedia of Angels, The Encyclopedia of Magic and Alchemy, The Encyclopedia of Saints, The Encyclopedia of Vampires, Werewolves, and Other Monsters,* and *The Encyclopedia of Witches and Witchcraft*, all from Facts On File. She lives in Maryland and her Web site is http://www.visionaryliving.com.